The Secondary Curriculum Design Handbook

Preparing Young Children for Their Futures

Brian Male and Mick Waters

continuum

Continuum International Publishing Group

The Tower Building   80 Maiden Lane
11 York Road   Suite 704
London SE1 7NX   New York NY 10038

www.continuumbooks.com

British Library Cataloguing-in-Publication Data
A catalogue record for this book is available from the British Library.

ISBN: 978-1-4411-0862-3 (paperback)
         978-1-4411-5998-4 (ePub)
         978-1-4411-1074-9 (PDF)

Library of Congress Cataloging-in-Publication Data
Male, Brian.
    The secondary curriculum design handbook : preparing our children for their futures / Brian Male and Mick Waters.
        p. cm.
    Includes bibliographical references and index.
    ISBN 978-1-4411-0862-3 – ISBN 978-1-4411-5998-4 – ISBN 978-1-4411-1074-9
1. Curriculum planning.   2. Education, Secondary–Curricula.   3. Curriculum planning–Great Britain.   4. Education, Secondary–Curricula–Great Britain.
I. Waters, Mick.   II. Title.

    LB2806.15.M338 2012
    375'.001–dc23

                                                2011048917

Typeset by Newgen Imaging Systems Pvt Ltd, Chennai, India
Printed and bound in Great Britain

The Secondary Curriculum
Design Handbook

A companion website to accompany this book is available online at:
http://education.male.continuumbooks.com
Please type in the URL above and receive your unique password for access
to the book's online resources.
If you experience any problems accessing the resources, please contact
Continuum at: info@continuumbooks.com

Also available from Continuum

Creating Tomorrow's Schools Today, Richard Gerver
Developing a Self-Evaluating School, Paul K. Ainsworth
The Primary Curriculum Design Handbook, Brian Male
School Improvement Through Drama, Patrice Baldwin
School and System Leadership, Susan Robinson

Contents

Foreword   vii

Introduction   1

SECTION I: How do we design a curriculum?

1   Curriculum design   7

2   A twenty-first century curriculum?   21

3   A framework for the curriculum   39

SECTION II: How do we organize learning?

4   The curriculum tree   51

5   The deep roots of learning   66

6   The canopy of leaves   80

7   Building in the competencies   96

8   Making learning irresistible   106

9   Local contexts   117

10   The timetable   127

11   Pathways and gateways   139

SECTION III: How will we know if we are successful?

12 Assessment and evaluation 157

SECTION IV: How do we get from here to there?

13 Managing institutional dimensions 177

14 A variety of options 191

15 Postscript – A world-class curriculum 198

Glossary 201

References 203

Index 207

Foreword

In response to the rapidly changing social and technological environment in which young people live, individual schools and whole countries are rethinking the curriculum in order to better equip young people for the present and especially for their future. Countries such as South Korea and Singapore – recognized as effective educators according to their place in international league tables – are reducing the amount of knowledge that young people have to learn in order to make room for more creativity in the curriculum. The government in England is reviewing the national curriculum with a view to slimming it down to a core of knowledge.

These developments give great opportunity for schools to redesign the curriculum that they offer to their learners. However, in many countries – including the three mentioned above – teachers have spent the last 20 or so years working under a detailed centrally directed curriculum that has left little room for them to be innovative. Now that governments are reducing the size of national curricula and asking teachers to use the new space to design a curriculum that is right for the students in their care, many teachers and school leaders are uncertain how to proceed. Having spent their whole career being told what to do by the government, they have forgotten – or, for more than half of the teaching profession, never known – how to design a curriculum.

Under these circumstances, this book could not be more timely. The school curriculum is much larger than the national curriculum and, with the latter shrinking, there is an increasing space for teachers and school leaders to design a curriculum that is exciting, engaging and relevant for all young people, responding to their natural curiosity and developing them as well-rounded individuals.

When a school designs its curriculum, it is setting out the very essence of its work. What do we want the young people who learn here to experience, to know, to be able to do? What sort of people are we trying to help them to become? What role does our school take in the process of helping the young people to grow? How do we prepare them for the life ahead of them; for work and for leisure; for an ever changing and challenging world?

This means not only organizing a body of knowledge – the national curriculum and whatever the school decides to add to it – into a coherent whole, but also deciding what skills and personal qualities are needed by the young people in the school, and how the development of these can be woven into the school curriculum.

The school curriculum is, as Mick Waters and Brian Male point out, the whole set of learning experiences in the school – timetabled lessons, assembly, pastoral care, using the library, sport, drama, music and other activities in which learners engage.

If the curriculum is, as the authors enticingly state, 'a feast of learning', then this book is a clear guide to show how schools can design a rich and varied menu. The authors bring their considerable experience to the challenge of helping each school to design the curriculum that matters for their students. They draw out the difference between curriculum design and curriculum planning and show how principles and values that underlie the work of teachers and school leaders can be the driving force for the learning in schools. The book draws on Mick's experience in local government and at the Qualifications and Curriculum Agency (QCA), and on Brian's work for UNESCO, to show how people across the world are thinking about how to make learning matter to children. Their deep commitment to education shines through in every chapter.

The Secondary Curriculum Design Handbook is readable and thought provoking, and prompts discussion and decision at every level in the school. The examples of learning, all from the time the authors have spent with teachers and students in schools, show the vitality of learning.

The content of the national curriculum is but one piece of the curriculum jigsaw, and this Handbook can be used alongside the developing national agenda to ensure that the principles of curriculum design are understood by everyone. The principles of a world class curriculum set out at the end of this book form an ambitious template against which schools can design a curriculum that is right for their students. That should always be our goal.

John Dunford
December 2011

Introduction

Think of the curriculum as a forecast of possibilities within an
arena of opportunities.
*– Carla Rinaldi, President of Reggio Studentren in Reggio Emilia,
Italy and professor at the University of Modena and Reggio
Emilia, quoted from a conference speech in London 2006.*

This is a curriculum design handbook, not a curriculum planning handbook.
Curriculum design is about all the things we want young people to learn; it
is also about creating all the experiences they need in order to learn those
things. It is about ensuring that those experiences are effective and compelling in themselves, and also that the sum total of those experiences adds up to
a coherent and worthwhile programme that will bring about the ends that we
seek. The accumulation of all these experiences is the curriculum itself.

This is a secondary school curriculum design handbook. The examples
are taken mainly from schools following the English National Curriculum
for Secondary Schools (Key Stages 3 and 4), but the principles of design apply
to any age and any country.

Schools around the world are struggling to balance the statutory requirements of a national curriculum and the need for students to attain good
grades in national examinations and qualifications with their desire to provide the wide, engaging and exciting curriculum that they know students
need to prepare them for life and work in the twenty-first century. Concerns
about standards often lead to a narrowing of the curriculum, and while many
schools have found their own solutions to these issues, many others lack the
confidence and the approach to curriculum design that would enable them
to resolve what seems like an impossible dilemma.

This dilemma is common in schools across the world, and is beginning to be recognized by national governments from China to Lithuania and Iraq, so the book has applications worldwide, although it is set mainly in an English context.

The book will be a practical guide to schools on how to design a curriculum that will engage students' interest, excite their imaginations, and at the same time provide them with the knowledge, skills and understanding they need in order achieve high standards and live and work successfully in the twenty-first century.

The secondary school is a time of huge change and development for students. They start as children and leave as young adults. It is a time for establishing the basis of attitudes and values, skills, knowledge and understanding that will last a lifetime. It is a time for students to establish their own identity as human beings, to find out how they relate to other people in a much wider society, and to begin to comprehend what it means to be a global citizen. It is a time for them to prepare themselves to take their place confidently in the adult world of work and responsibilities, of leisure, fulfilment and opportunity. It is a time to explore and make connections between the accumulated knowledge and wisdom of all those humans who have gone before them; a time to be inducted into the major systems of human thought and understanding; a time when direct experiences are put together into conceptual development; a time to develop imaginatively and creatively; a time to be excited, challenged and inspired; a time to lay down the roots to lifelong learning.

Curriculum design is about how we can construct a curriculum that will match these aspirations.

This book is being published just as the English National Curriculum is under review. So some English schools might consider this to be an inopportune time to be thinking about the curriculum at all: What's the point of thinking about the curriculum when they are going to change it anyway? But there is a very good reason for doing so.

The curriculum of schools is much more than a national curriculum. Schools are rich in learning, much of which goes way beyond any national curriculum, and there is a set of principles and approaches that will take a curriculum way beyond the ordinary and sufficient, and make it truly 'world-class'. These principles and approaches apply in any country whatever the national curriculum. They take learning beyond the national and towards the universal. They will enable schools to incorporate the revised national expectations into a truly inspiring curriculum for students.

These world-class principles are about the way any country's national curriculum is turned into learning experiences for students that are exciting and uplifting, that recognize the individuality of every student, and that encourage their development as human beings. These principles underpin this book, and provide a way in which the curriculum can be made engaging and inspiring whatever the national curriculum is, or turns out to be. The principles are about how schools can add value to national expectations and locate them in a setting that is both local and global.

These principles can be applied to the present English National Curriculum, and to any new one that might be devised. They can be applied to the national curriculum of any country, and provide a way of taking national requirements and using them to create learning that is exciting, coherent and fulfilling; learning that will prepare young people for the twenty-first century.

This is not an academic book, although it is based on research and makes reference to it. It is a practical book for curriculum designers. It does not provide a ready-made, off the peg or off the web curriculum that will apply to all schools. But it provides a route to designing a curriculum that can challenge and inspire all learners.

It sees the role of the teacher as more than a deliverer of someone else's curriculum, more than technicians rehashing someone else's recipes. We must unleash the power of the curriculum by enabling teachers to be curriculum designers who create learning experiences that excite and engage young people; experiences that are rooted in their present understandings, but that widen their horizons and raise their aspirations.

Schools have the key role in curriculum design, for it is they who must bridge the gap between on the one hand the flexibility that is necessary to ensure that the curriculum builds on what students have just learned and responds to their developing interests and needs, and on the other hand the need to provide a coherent curriculum over the 5 years of compulsory secondary education. It is not governments but schools that can ensure that the curriculum excites imaginations and provides inspiration. Schools can make the curriculum a feast of learning that no student can resist.

We need a curriculum with a strong moral purpose; a curriculum that we all came into the profession to teach. If we get this right, we can send every young person out into adulthood with the confidence, the ability and the desire to make the world a better place.

SECTION I

How do we design a curriculum?

1 Curriculum design

The Statue

Year 9 students had been set a task to find out about a local historical character who had been important in the anti-slavery movement, but of whom the students had never heard. Having completed their research and visited the house near the school where she had lived, the students were indignant that she was not more famous. 'There ought to be a statue of her', they said. The matter might have rested there if the teacher had not challenged them, 'So what are you going to do about it, then?'

They thought the mayor must be in charge of statues, so they wrote to him. He was sympathetic to the idea and could probably find a site, but said that he was not sure about the budget – how much would it cost? The students then looked up local sculptors and found out how to go about commissioning a statue; a complex process needing designs and specifications, many on-site meetings, artistic talks about style and 'historical resonance' and sharp discussions about the budget.

These initial soundings produced a rough costing and the mayor agreed to find half the funding (times were easier then!) if the students could find the other half. They then set about raising money from events and donations. They set up a website for publicity and an account into which donations could be paid, contacted local businesses and societies and organized events including a play that they devised themselves. They made a video to go with requests for donations and filmed the mayor and other public figures appealing for funds.

The feeling of pride and achievement in those young people when the statue was finally unveiled was immense. One day they may take their grandchildren to see it and will say, 'I did that!'

All too frequently, the secondary school curriculum has become constrained by a variety of external pressures such as examination syllabuses, qualifications, vocational education and a variety of national requirements. Instead of unleashing the excitement and curiosity of young people, the curriculum can become a seemingly endless list of things to get through. This book is about how we can create an exciting, engaging and spontaneous curriculum, and at the same time ensure that students achieve high standards in public examinations and attain the qualifications they need. This sounds like the Holy Grail of Education. Is it possible to design such a curriculum?

And what does the tree on the cover of this book have to do with curriculum design? Read on.

What does the statue story above have to do with a book about designing a curriculum? Surely these are 'extra-curricular' activities, and so not part of the curriculum at all? But when you think about it, an amazing amount of learning is packed into this: history, art, information and communication technology (ICT), maths, drama, English and citizenship. What might be different here is the way in which these things were learned. None of the learning was explicitly planned by the teacher in advance, and very little took place in 'lessons'. Yet it is all part of these young people's experiences. And it was there by design. Designed, but not planned.

More than planning

Curriculum design is about more than listing all the things we want students to learn; it is also about designing the experiences that students need in order to learn those things. It is about ensuring that those experiences are effective and compelling in themselves, and also that the sum total of those experiences adds up to a coherent and worthwhile programme that will bring about the outcomes that we want.

The curriculum is the whole set of learning experiences that students are involved in as they move through the school.

There are three levels of understanding the curriculum:

1. The curriculum as set out by the nation: all those things the nation thinks our young people should learn.
2. The curriculum as set out by the school or the teacher: the mediation of those national expectations into a form that is relevant to the particular students in the school or class.
3. The curriculum as experienced by the students: this might vary from student to student even within a class.

The first two levels impact on the third. We need to consider all three levels, but what really counts is what the students actually learn.

More than the national curriculum or the examination syllabus

The nation sets out what it wants its students to learn in a national curriculum. The school interprets this and sets out what it wants its students to learn in its curriculum plans. But success depends on what the students make of all this: it is their set of experiences that determines what they will learn. And this can vary from student to student even within the same class or lesson, because they all bring something different to their learning, and are building on a different past set of experiences. They are all seeking to make sense of new information in the light of their present understanding, and that present understanding will vary from student to student.

The curriculum of every school is much more than the national curriculum – whatever country you are in. A national curriculum prescribes a common set of learning to which all students are entitled. But these expectations are always mediated by the school itself, and each school responds to national expectations in its own way – even if they all think they are responding in the same way. And the national expectations need to be placed in the local context and presented in such a way that they make sense to the particular set of students. The national expectations are always achieved within a local setting. But what are these national expectations and how do we build them into the curriculum?

More than the subjects and programmes of study

What students learn in any school goes way beyond the subjects on the timetable. They are learning all the time, whether we want them to or not, and by the age of 16 they are very different people from the 11-year-olds who started in Year 7. This breadth of learning is often reflected in our schools' aims, which almost always refer to aspects of personal, social and emotional development, and to a range of skills.

The set of national aims for the English Secondary Curriculum reflects this breadth – young people should become:

- Successful learners
- Confident individuals
- Responsible citizens

These aims may well disappear as statutory obligations in the review of the curriculum that is under way at the time of writing (see the website that accompanies this book for updates), but most other countries, and schools in England, see these sorts of aims as important anyway, and would wish to pursue them. Most schools therefore have a range of programmes for personal and social development and for 'key' or 'generic' skills that apply across the curriculum.

Personal and social development

Most countries make reference to personal and social development in their national curricula and some set specific targets. In England, the Early Years Foundation Stage (EYFS) guidance for children up to the age of 5 details aspects of personal development, but there is no corresponding statutory section in either the primary or secondary national curriculum. Perhaps it was thought that children will have finished developing personally by the age of 5. Perhaps it was thought that students' personal development is not the business of secondary schools. However, it is part of the non-statutory guidance for Personal, Social and Health Education at Key Stages 3 and 4, and most schools and parents see it as an important part of the work of the school. It is also an important aspect of the three aims.

Key skills

Most countries also refer to a range of skills that apply across subjects and go beyond them. These might be general, such as critical thinking, problem solving, communicating or investigating, or they might be more specific such as analysing, synthesizing and evaluating. Since they apply across the curriculum, these are often referred to as *generic skills* or *key skills*. The English National Curriculum for secondary education was published alongside a set of six Personal, Learning and Thinking Skills (PLTS) that were seen as supporting the three aims. The PLTS are those that enable young people to become:

- Self-managers
- Teamworkers
- Creative thinkers
- Reflective learners

- Effective participants
- Independent enquirers

If we take these sorts of skills seriously, then they will have significant implications for the curriculum and for the nature of learning within it.

More than knowledge

Within the subjects themselves, there can be a tension between subject knowledge, skills and understanding. These three terms have always been used in the English National Curriculum to denote different forms of learning:

1. *Knowledge* is the possession of information.
2. A *skill* is the ability to perform an operation (either mental or physical). It is basically the ability to do something.
3. *Understanding* goes beyond knowledge into a comprehension of general principles that allow pieces of knowledge to be fitted into a structure. These structures are often referred to as 'concepts'.

Much of the debate about the importance of knowledge arises because the term 'knowledge' is used in a variety of ways in education: from 'knowing that' (simple information to be recalled) to 'knowing how to' (which implies skills) and 'knowing about' (which implies understanding). There is general agreement that conceptual development (understanding) is at the deepest level of learning.

A simple example would be a student learning about capital cities. The ability to recall that Paris is the capital city of France is a piece of knowledge. The ability to find out what a country's capital city is if you did not already know would involve a skill (using an atlas or the internet). Explaining why one city rather than another is the capital (Why is Sydney not the capital of Australia?) involves understanding the concept of capitals. There is a further dimension to learning: the extent of your knowledge about capitals (depth as well as range).

It is important to note two things here: first, the distinction between knowledge, skills and understanding is key to curriculum design because they each involve a different type of learning that the curriculum needs to take account of, and, second, the curriculum must equip young people with more than knowledge. A curriculum without skills or understanding would be pointlessly shallow. It would be the curriculum of the pub quiz. A curriculum without knowledge would be equally pointless, and it would also be impossible!

Putting them together: competencies

When education is successful, learners are able to make use of the knowledge, understanding and skills they have acquired because they have developed the right attitudes and approaches to use them effectively. This coming together of knowledge, understanding, skills and personal development is usually referred to as a 'competency'.

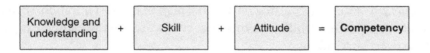

Many countries make use of this concept in developing their curricula. For example, Singapore's national curriculum (and remember that Singapore always does well on international comparisons) has at its heart: Social and Emotional Competencies and Twenty-first Century Competencies. Singapore's twenty-first century competencies are listed as:

- Civic literacy
- Global awareness
- Cross-curricular skills
- Critical and media skills
- Information and communication skills

The key to curriculum design is how these three aspects – subject knowledge, personal development and key skills – can be brought together for their mutual benefit and to achieve competency. It is not a matter of 'either subjects or skills'. It is both – and personal development as well. At the heart of curriculum design is the methodology for putting these together.

More than lessons

The main reason why a school's curriculum is inevitably broader than a national curriculum is that most curriculum planning focuses on what goes on in lessons, but students do not learn only in lessons. They learn from the *routines* of the school, the things that happen every day or week such as changing library books, going to assembly, lunchtimes and breaks, performing duties, playing for teams, organizing activities. Some of these routines can be rich sources of learning. The work around the statue became a routine for the Year 9 students in the opening scenario. Sometimes schools are oblivious to all this learning and it can even run counter to their intentions. In other cases, they build it into their design and channel the learning profitably.

In addition to the routines, schools frequently organize *events*: things that do not happen every day or week. These can be of long continuous duration such as a residential visit or an Arts Week, or a series of experiences over a long period of time like putting on a school play, or of short duration, such as a visit to a museum. Unlike the routines, events are usually planned as part of the overt curriculum.

There are also all those things that happen *outside normal hours*. They may not involve all the students all the time, but a huge amount of learning takes place in clubs, societies, sports, music groups, school councils, environment committees and the like. These are seldom part of the planned curriculum, but are another rich source of learning.

There is also the *ethos* of the school and the set of *relationships* that prevail. These are not part of the planned curriculum, but will impact on it, especially when the list of things we want students to learn includes things like: 'show respect', or 'be sensitive to others' or 'be tolerant and sensitive to others' needs'. This can impact on the school as a 'learning community' in which both adults and other students contribute to learning (Lave & Wenger 1991).

The point is not that a full curriculum *should* look like this, but that the curriculum of a school *inevitably* looks like this. There will be very few schools indeed where all these things do not go on. It is just that we tend to focus on the lessons. If we were to draw a map of the things that make up the curriculum, the map might look something like Figure 1.1.

Do these things go on in your school? Are there other things, too? What would the relative size of the different boxes be in your school?

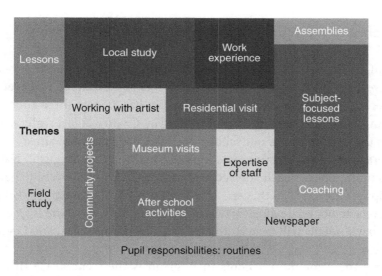

Figure 1.1 The school curriculum

(You don't need to do this exactly with a calendar and stopwatch – just note down your overall impression.) Would the map be the same for each year group? Is this the best ratio for producing the learning you want? Would it be the same for all subjects? How would we resolve any differences?

Of course, learning does not happen in separate boxes. The impact on students is an holistic one. If we can get our curriculum design right, we can harness the power of all these apparently separate boxes to maximize the learning of each student. We need to break down the walls to benefit from the flow of learning.

In most schools, lessons tend to be the main vehicle of learning; but lessons come in a wide variety of forms. It is essential to consider these as part of curriculum design, and we shall do so in later chapters. But curriculum design also needs to take into account the totality of learning in the school, the balance between the different elements and which type of learning experience is most suited to promoting different kinds of learning. All of this impacts on whether our curriculum is successful in bringing about the ends that we seek. This, in turn, brings us to the first of the three design questions, and until we know the answer to this question we cannot expect to be able to design a worthwhile curriculum. What ends are we seeking? (If this is the first design question, what are the other two?)

What are we trying to achieve?

You might think that there is no point in asking such a question because we have a national curriculum, and our job is to teach it, or to 'cover' it or 'deliver' it. The English National Curriculum has its own three aims, so we all know what we are trying to achieve anyway. Or do we? Is it really so clear-cut? Is the curriculum of our schools really focused on those aims?

There are also Attainment Targets within the English National Curriculum; one for each subject, set out in eight helpful levels. (There is a descriptor for each level that sets out the expected attainment for that level. The levels do not relate directly to year groups or ages, but there is an expectation that students will have attained Level 4 by the age of 11, and Level 6 by the age of 14.)

Above these for most schools in England is the General Certificate of Secondary Education (GCSE) public examination at the age of 16. And then there are the Advanced Level ('A' Level) public examinations for those who stay on until they are 18. These are often the real goals for schools and for students and their parents as well. The focus on these becomes relentless, not only because they are the gateways to employment and to higher education, but because school performance is measured by them. League tables are published of these examination results and school inspections are based on them.

Yet employers often complain that even though a student may leave school with five good passes at GCSE, they do not have the range of skills needed for employment. They may have gained high marks in a test, but they still do not communicate effectively in a range of situations, think for themselves, act with initiative, co-operate well in teams, show empathy for a customer or stick at a difficult task. Their schooling and curriculum have not prepared them properly for their adult life.

So we are back to the dilemma with which we started. How can we have a curriculum that enables students to do well in the examinations that are so important to them, while also developing the range of competencies that they need? Do we need to abandon our wider aims?

This book will argue that it is not a matter of having either one thing or another; it can be both. We do not have to choose between 'noble aims' or GCSE passes. In fact, it is when we take account of our aims and use them as a basis for design that the curriculum starts to fall into place, and so does students' learning.

The three circles

The American business guru Simon Sinek talks about building successful companies. You can see his 'TED' talk on www.ted.com/simonsinek. In this talk, he shows three concentric circles labelled 'Why?', 'How?' and 'What?' 'Why' is at the centre (see Figure 1.2). Sinek argues that most companies spend their time focusing on *what* it is that they produce, and little time thinking about *how* their product is different from and better than their rival's. Few ask themselves *why* they are in business at all. He suggests that really successful companies like Apple draw their success from starting with the 'Why'. In Apple's case it is to make information and communication technology easy to use, attractive and intuitive, supportive of what the then CEO Steve Jobs called the 'Liberal Arts'. Apple then ask how they can do that: by making simple devices that are good to look at and to hold, that have very few buttons, and that run software that doesn't need a huge instruction book to use. That brings them to *what* they need to produce: ipods, iphones and ipads. The 'What' is really good because they started with the 'Why'.

Sinek extends his analysis to really successful communicators and movements. He talks about figures such as Martin Luther King who had a really strong 'Why'. King didn't start with the 'What' and so decide to organize protests and sit-ins and make speeches, and then wonder *how* he could organize them and *why* he needed demonstrations anyway. He started with the 'Why' and everything else fell into place. Half a million people turned up in Washington on a day in March 1968, even though the event was never

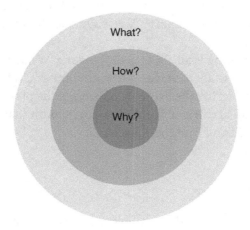

Figure 1.2 The three circles

advertised and no one had Facebook. Sinek points out that Martin Luther King had a dream, not a business plan.

Sinek also argues that the answer to the commercial 'Why' is not: 'To make money'. This is essential to an understanding of this analysis. He suggests that making money is the *outcome* of getting all the other bits right, and that companies that start only with a desire to make money and then wonder *what* they can do to make it, seldom succeed. If the main driver for an organization is to make money, then product quality and customer satisfaction are compromised and the company is less successful. The ipod and iphone are really successful because they spring from the ideal of beautiful, intuitive technology. This drives the product design; the designers, not the accountants, are in charge; and as a result the accountants are happy.

Sinek does not apply his analysis to schools and the curriculum, but the comparison is clear to see. When you think about it, most curriculum planning in schools is about the 'What'. We spend our time thinking about *what* it is that we want the students to learn. We are in the outer circle. Planning meetings are often about taking the Programmes of Study and organizing them into schemes and lessons to answer the questions, 'What have we got to cover?' and 'What are we going to teach?' Then we spend a bit of time thinking about *how* we are going to teach the 'What'. But we seldom get to the 'Why', which is at the centre of things. 'Why do we want them to learn these things in the first place?'

And Sinek's key point also applies to education. A* at GCSE is not the 'Why' of education, but if we get the curriculum right, then such success will be the outcome. In fact, a school is much more likely to be successful in terms of the GCSE if it starts with the 'Why'. The Office for Standards in Education, Children's Services and Skills (Ofsted) has good evidence of this in England in their Ofsted report 'Twelve Outstanding Secondary Schools' (ref. 080240 (2009)).

Curriculum Planning is all about arranging the 'What' in the outer circle. Curriculum Design is about starting from the inner circle, and arriving at the 'What' by considering the 'How'. It is through the process of curriculum design that we shall arrive at a world-class curriculum that enables students to explore the world and find their place in it.

The statue

It is because the school in the example was clear about the 'Why' that it was able to accommodate all the work that went into commissioning the statue, and did not worry about whether the time students spent on it would detract from the rest of the curriculum. The school saw it as part of the curriculum, and could see how the experience could include learning in key aspects of the programmes.

It was not planned long in advance because the idea of the statue came spontaneously from the students themselves. The school did not know it was going to happen, but was able to respond to this because its system was planned around the 'Why' and 'How', rather than being focused on the 'What'. This approach gave the teachers the flexibility to draw upon the elements of the 'What' within developing situations. They were confident enough to be flexible and take advantage of rich learning situations, because they were clear about their aims and had a system to ensure that the flexible curriculum would be coherent and balanced overall.

It also involved a co-operative approach in which teachers from a range of subjects were able to recognize an opportunity that arose and then adapt their programmes to take advantage of it. It involved a flexibility of school organization that allowed these students time to pursue this project. It involved confidence that the time spent would contribute to the school's overall goals and so be worthwhile.

We often talk to students about citizenship, but it is not easy to put them into a situation where they are able to make real-life decisions for the greater good, and experience this aspect of citizenship first hand. The statue provided just such an opportunity. The richness of learning was in the experience itself, but was brought out by the school's ability to allow it to develop. The confidence came from a system that was not all about arranging 'content', but was about the deeper goals.

More than the first chapter

This first chapter has attempted to put the curriculum into a wider context. It is more than the national curriculum and involves more than lessons, subjects and knowledge (although it involves all of those). It is about key aims and a system of design that is more than curriculum planning. It is about the set of experiences that students need in order to learn the things we want them to learn to equip them for the journey of life. If we want them to acquire knowledge, skills and understanding as well as to develop personally, emotionally, socially and morally as human beings, then that set of experiences needs to be rich and varied.

The statue was an example of rich learning that involved skills and understanding as well as knowledge; that enabled students to develop personal and social skills and to engage as citizens. It is an example of learning beyond the national curriculum, learning beyond lessons, beyond subjects and beyond knowledge. Not all learning can be like that, but when some learning is like that, it can make an impact across the curriculum, and take it beyond the ordinary. It can take the students beyond the ordinary and start to open up the world for them.

We now go beyond the first chapter, and open up the rest of the book to look in more detail at what would make a curriculum extraordinary.

In case you hadn't worked it out, the three design questions are:

1. What are we trying to achieve?
2. How should we organize learning most effectively to achieve those things?
3. How will we know if we have been successful?

2 A twenty-first century curriculum?

The Michelin Starred Restaurant

The kitchen of a Michelin starred restaurant is typically busy and tense. These kitchens often seem to be staffed by impossibly young people, but the ones here are even younger than usual. The menu is extensive and the restaurant is, as always, packed.

The kitchen staff have been involved in planning the menu from the point of view of quality and nutrition, pricing the ingredients, ensuring it can be done within the budget, arranging the necessary portion control and planning the preparation and cooking sequence so that the meals will all come together at the required time. They are hyper-aware of safety and hygiene, working as they are with sharp utensils and intense heat, and responsible as they are for the health of the customers.

The waiting staff are also younger than usual, but are well versed in their roles, knowledgeable about the menus and the wines, able to greet and talk to customers appropriately, able to lay tables sumptuously and serve with flair and with care. They have designed the menus and arranged advertising for the day.

You will have guessed that all the restaurant staff are from the local secondary school. This is the day when the restaurant gives itself over to students to prepare and serve a meal for local pensioners. The programme has been running for some years. The restaurant puts its considerable reputation on the line, and finds that the students always repay the faith placed in them.

Here we are in the second decade of the twenty-first century and people are still wondering if we have a curriculum that fully prepares our young people to live successfully in it. People are asking this question all around the world, and some countries are taking particular steps to ensure that their curricula respond to the new challenges.

In England, the question about a twenty-first century curriculum is particularly pertinent. The review of the whole national curriculum announced in 2011 is based on the premise that 'We intend to restore the National Curriculum to its original purpose – a minimum national entitlement for all our young people organised around the subject disciplines.' These subject disciplines around which the curriculum is to be organized for the twenty-first century bear a remarkable similarity to the national curriculum set out by the Revised Code of 1905 (see Table 2.1).

Can you spot the difference? No prizes for this one: The names have changed, but beyond that, information technology is in, and housewifery is out. There are, no doubt, some people who regret the omission of housewifery.

The world that young people entered on leaving school in 1905 was very different from the world as it is now. In England, they came out into a fairly static Edwardian society where they worked in occupations such as agriculture, manufacturing, mining, commerce or administration – or they became housewives – and expected to do the same job in pretty much the same way for the rest of their lives. The curriculum of that time was calculated to prepare them for that static sort of world.

Table 2.1 The developing curriculum

1905	1989
Reading and writing	English
Arithmetic	Mathematics
Nature study	Science
History	History
Geography	Geography
Drawing	Art
Physical exercise	Physical Education
Singing	Music
Manual training	Design and Technology
Housewifery	Information Technology

The second decade of the twenty-first century is a very different place, and in particular it is a lot less static. It is expected that people will change jobs several times in their working life, and not just from one employer to another, but taking on fundamentally different occupations. It is predicted that in 25 years time over half the jobs people will be doing have not yet been invented. And, of course, many young people will struggle to find jobs at all. How do we prepare our young people for such a world? This is not to suggest that education is only there to prepare young people for employment; the changes and challenges are widespread and affect all aspects of personal life as well.

It is not necessary to labour this point here. We all know the extraordinary recent rate of technological change and the impact this has on employment and on society in general. We could add to that such factors as globalization, the changing balance of economic and political power from the West to the East, changing social and economic patterns and climate change. The impact is not just on employment, it is also on social patterns and private lives. Who would have thought 20 years ago that the seemingly major form of social interaction between young people would be through a handheld electronic device?

So, if the twenty-first century is so different from 1905, will the same set of subjects suffice to prepare our young people for the life ahead of them? If we need something different, what is it: a different set of subjects, changes within the subjects? Or is it something else?

What do young people need to learn in order to succeed in the twenty-first century?

When the former Qualifications and Curriculum Authority (QCA) started the review of the English National Curriculum for secondary schools in 2005, it asked a wide range of people this very question. It asked parents, teachers, governors, employers, faith groups, the wider public and students themselves.

In all these groups, all over the country, from backgrounds as diverse as from the Confederation of British Industry (CBI) to the local parish councillors, the list was remarkably similar:

Young people need to:

- Be creative
- Communicate well
- Be literate and numerate
- Solve problems
- Work together in teams
- Have a global perspective
- Show initiative
- Work independently
- Be a life-long learner

Do you agree with that list? What would you add, or take away? Are there any surprises?

It is interesting that in all those different groups surveyed by the QCA in England, nobody said that what young people really needed was 5A*–C passes at GCSE. Everyone listed wider skills, attitudes and dispositions that they saw as equipping a young person for the future. It is also interesting that nobody mentioned particular subjects either. Yet it is the subjects that form the basis of most of what goes on in schools and are the statutory basis of the English National Curriculum. Perhaps everyone took the subjects for granted so didn't bother to list them. Perhaps the questions were 'loaded', encouraging people to think of higher or wider aspirations. Or perhaps people saw the things on the list as more important than subjects. Perhaps we do not have to choose between high attainment in subjects and wider aims.

Whatever the reason, meeting after meeting and group after group came up with similar lists that go beyond subjects. And most of the things on the list above are very similar to Singapore's '21st Century Competencies'.

In an effort to focus on this impact, the QCA conducted its wide consultations by asking people to draw a successful learner, and then write around the picture the factors for success in the twenty-first century. People were invited to look at their list and ask 'Which of the things on the list are skills?' 'Which are knowledge, and which are qualities?' Lines were then drawn linking knowledge to the brain, skills to the hand and qualities to the heart. This may not be anatomically correct, but it presents a strong visual image.

In almost every case, most of the things people wanted students to learn led to the heart. Yet, most of the planned curriculum is to do with the brain.

It is a useful exercise to carry out within a school with staff or with governors and parents. It not only promotes discussion about some key aims and aspirations, it helps focus on the differing nature of learning within a curriculum, and raises questions about what should be the basis of curriculum design.

Common around the world

Interestingly, people's view of what young people need to prepare them for the twenty-first century seems to be the same all over the world. The same exercise has been repeated in many countries, and the results are very similar. The first picture in Figure 2.1 was drawn in Leeds, and you will no doubt recognize the language in the second picture and so will see that people in Lithuania say exactly the same thing.

In almost all cases, people respond to their perceptions of the changing world of the twenty-first century. This is why they rate the importance of such attributes as confidence, flexibility and resilience (darbstus and smalsus). They also recognize that successful young people will need to be active

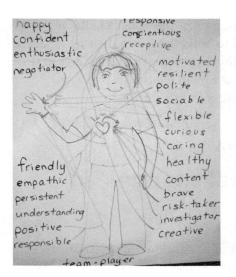 

Figure 2.1 A successful learner

The curriculum must respond to the changing knowledge and skills needs in society and in the world economy.

It must develop the capacity for high quality life-long learning.

Figure 2.2 Finland

The curriculum must reflect the economic and social changes associated with the development of our global, knowledge-based world and their implications for our economy and society.

Figure 2.3 Victoria

rather than passive, so they see the need to be enthusiastic and brave risk takers, and investigators (drasus and linksmas). There is worldwide recognition that individualism will not be a sufficient quality for the twenty-first century, and that co-operation and teamwork will be necessary. Other common features across the world are creativity, communication, problem solving and critical thinking.

Taking account of wider challenges

Many countries around the world recognize the wider challenges of the twenty-first century and have sought to build these into their national curricula. For example, let us see what Finland (a country that features near the top of most international comparisons) says in Figure 2.2.
Also, let us see what Victoria, Australia, says in Figure 2.3.

So how are countries reflecting the 'economic and social changes' in their curricula?

Almost every country that has revised its national curriculum recently has added a range of skills along with the aspects of personal development

Singapore		
	Social and emotional competencies	21st century competencies
	• Self-awareness • Self-management • Social awareness • Relationship management • Responsible decision making	• Civic literacy • Global awareness • Cross-curricular skills • Critical and media skills • Information and communication skills

Figure 2.4 Singapore competencies

New Zealand
 Key competencies
• Thinking • Using languages, symbols and texts • Managing self • Relating to others

Figure 2.5 New Zealand competencies

that we looked at in Chapter 1. They see these as augmenting the subject areas, adding a new dimension to them and to learning overall. We have already mentioned the two sets of competencies in the Singapore curriculum (although these are not all competencies in the strictest definition) (see Figure 2.4).

New Zealand also has a set of Key Competencies that operate across the curriculum, which is given in Figure 2.5.

The United Nations Educational, Scientific and Cultural Organisation (UNESCO) in 2009 identified four '21st Century Competencies' (Ananiadou & Claro 2009) and recommended them to member nations as needing to underpin all curricula. These competencies are the 'Four Cs' of:

1. Communication

2. Critical thinking and problem solving

3. Collaboration

4. Creativity

UNESCO helped to develop a national curriculum for the new nation of Kosovo, and six different sorts of competencies have been identified within that curriculum (see Figure 2.6).

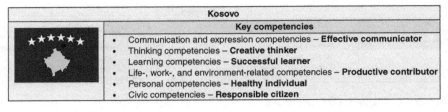

Kosovo	
Key competencies	
	• Communication and expression competencies – **Effective communicator** • Thinking competencies – **Creative thinker** • Learning competencies – **Successful learner** • Life-, work-, and environment-related competencies – **Productive contributor** • Personal competencies – **Healthy individual** • Civic competencies – **Responsible citizen**

Figure 2.6 Kosovo competencies

England		
	Three aims	**Personal, learning and thinking skills (PLTS)**
	• Successful learners • Confident individuals • Reponsible citizens	• Independent enquirers • Effective participants • Reflective learners • Team workers • Self managers • Creative thinkers

Figure 2.7 England – secondary skills

And what about England?

If you are familiar with the English National Curriculum, you might be thinking that the Kosovo list looks rather familiar (see Figure 2.7).

Did UNESCO look at the English example? The element that is present in Kosovo but not in the English aims or PLTS is communication. Interestingly, neither numeracy nor ICT is in either list. Are these in any way essential to functioning in the twenty-first century?

The Rose Review of the English National Primary Curriculum in 2010 identified a key element of essential literacy, numeracy and ICT that underpinned and unlocked learning in all other subjects. In a sense, these seem rather like the functional skills in English secondary education.

Functional skills

A set of functional skills in literacy, numeracy and ICT was developed in 2007 as stand-alone qualifications and also as:

- a component of the new Foundation, Higher and Advanced Diplomas,
- part of all Foundation Learning programmes,

- a component in apprenticeship frameworks,
- elements of English, mathematics and ICT GCSEs.

The 'functionality' of these skills lies in their application in practical situations. This was seen as distinguishing them from *all* of literacy, numeracy and ICT, which might be studied in an academic way or for their own sake. The framework of skills was set out at different levels from Entry to Level 2 on the National Qualifications Framework (NQF) and Qualifications and Credit Framework (QCF) where Level 2 is the equivalent of a good GCSE pass. However, the notion was somewhat clouded because the levels leant heavily on the Level Descriptions of the national curriculum subjects without any clear criteria of where the functional skills stopped and the rest of the subject began.

The Rose review stripped away the notion of levels and defined the 'essentialness' or functionality as those elements that were necessary for the study or understanding of other subjects, and for everyday life. In this definition, the study of Shakespeare's plays is important, and appreciating them is life-enhancing. The same could be said of Beethoven's music. But neither is 'essential' in any functional sense.

The 'essentialness' comes from the need to use these skills in contexts other than the subjects in which they are normally located. For example, you need to be able to read in order to access learning in almost any other subject, and in order to function as a twenty-first century citizen. Similarly, you need to be able to speak and to understand what other people are saying to you. You need a level of numeracy in order to access other subjects too. Everything from science to physical education (PE) has an element of number, measurement, data handling and shape. It would be difficult to function adequately as a citizen without a minimum level of numeracy. And it has become essential to have a level of competence in information technology. What makes these essential is their functionality. They enable you to learn other things, and are essential to be able to function competently in the twenty-first century.

The notion of functional skills (like essential English, numeracy and ICT) is significant to curriculum design because as well as having applications across the curriculum, they are aspects of subjects (English, maths and ICT), unlike the more general skills such as 'thinking' or 'decision making', which are skills that are not located within any subject area. There is a further set of skills used within the English secondary curriculum that combines the two.

OCR Key Skills

The six 'Key Skills' identified by the Oxford, Cambridge and RSA examination boards (OCR) are:

1. Communication
2. Application of number
3. ICT
4. Improving own learning performance
5. Problem solving
6. Working with others

The first three are similar to 'essential' or 'functional' literacy, numeracy and ICT, while the last three can be found within the PLTS. They also bear a close resemblance to the sets seen across the world from Singapore to Kosovo.

A response to the twenty-first century

As we look at other countries, we see that they are responding to the challenges of the present century by adding a range of skills and competencies, and aspects of personal development, to their national curricula. This does not mean that they have abandoned subjects, or that they do not see them as important, but that they see the need for the curriculum to go beyond them in order to enable young people to cope with life in the twenty-first century. There is a widespread recognition that the learning contained within the set of subjects that may have served people well in 1905 will be insufficient to equip people for the world our young people face a century later.

The rise of computer technology is only one aspect of the change, but it is one with a significant impact on learning itself and the way in which we view the world (Heppell 2004). We are still at the beginning of understanding the implications for schools and the curriculum (Facer 2003), and the implications for the way in which students' learning is developing (Pahl 2005, Goswami & Bryant 2007).

The range of things added falls into two of the three categories we considered in Chapter 1: Personal Development and Key Skills (subject knowledge was the third). To these we have now added the new category of the 'essential' or 'functional' literacy, numeracy and ICT discussed above.

They all have significant implications for curriculum design, and we shall take them one at a time.

Personal development

The QCA consultation on what young people need to equip them for the twenty-first century listed mainly aspects of personal development, rather than elements of knowledge and understanding within the subject domains. The competencies listed by countries revising their national curricula also contain many aspects of personal development. These aspects fall into several categories that have significant implications for curriculum design.

Some elements of personal development are skills. A skill is the ability to perform a physical or mental operation. As such, skills can be learned and can to some extent be taught. They generally need practice through the performance of the skill itself, rather than reading about the skill or listening to someone explaining it. This can be seen in a physical skill such as hitting a ball with a tennis racquet; you can watch any number of demonstrations, but you only learn the skill by hitting the ball yourself. The same is true of mental skills; they have to be performed to be acquired.

Some of the other aspects of personal development on the lists are not skills that can be learned or practised in this way, but are attitudes, values, qualities and dispositions. For example, 'self-confidence' is not a skill than can be taught, but is a quality that is developed through a particular set of experiences (usually those where some success was achieved). To 'show initiative' would be a disposition as it is a tendency to act in a particular way. This tendency may be the result of the possession of certain skills, but is not a skill in itself. To be 'caring' or 'curious' would seem to be more like an attitude.

You may well disagree with specifics here and think, for instance, that 'caring' is a value rather than an attitude. There is no overall consensus in this area; many of these categories overlap and there is no clear agreement on where one ends and another begins. In fact, some people do not see them as categories at all, but as part of a continuum of personal development.

However, it is critically important for a curriculum designer to give thought to the sort of experiences that would promote the different aspects of personal development. It is no good expecting students to develop skills without opportunities to try them out and practise them, and it is equally pointless expecting students to develop attitudes simply by being told to do so.

This does not mean that the desired attitudes, values, qualities and dispositions or anything else on the continuum cannot be promoted through the curriculum. Indeed, it is important that they should be promoted. But they tend to be the outcome of a long series of experiences rather than things that can be taught discretely, like Venn diagrams or the formation of ox-bow lakes.

If attitudes, values, qualities and dispositions are the result of a whole series of experiences, then we need to give thought to the totality of the experiences students undergo in our schools. In Chapter 1 we looked at the way in which learning does not just occur in lessons but through such things as the routines of the school, events and through the ethos and relationships that prevail. These are of critical importance to a whole range of personal development aspects, especially the ethos and relationships. These aspects of personal development are long-term and the result of the whole experience that each student receives through school. Of course, students are in school for a relatively short proportion of each week and year, and there will be other influences on their personal development, but schools can still be very influential, in both positive and negative ways.

Within the lists, there are personal skills that need to be built specifically into the curriculum. These would include working collaboratively, self-management, working independently, managing feelings, adapting behaviour to others and negotiating. Some of these might be seen as personal or emotional skills, and some as social skills. They can be structured directly into the curriculum and improved through practice. We shall consider how best to do this in Chapter 4.

Thinking and learning skills

Not all the OCR Key Skills or PLTS of the English curriculum are aspects of personal development. Many are skills that relate more to the cognitive domain, and that can be applied across the curriculum. These are sometimes referred to as Thinking and Learning Skills as they are important to learning across the curriculum. They are the cognitive skills that enable students to make sense of all the information they find out about the world, because these skills apply across all human knowledge, and so across the curriculum. Some countries, such as Singapore, refer to them as 'cross-curricular skills'. In its co-development work with schools, QCA identified five such skills that tend to occur in lists of most countries and that broadly subsume the rest:

1. Investigate

2. Analyse and synthesize

3. Create and develop

4. Evaluate

5. Communicate

These are similar to UNESCO's '21st Century Competencies' (critical thinking, creativity, communication and collaboration) minus the 'social' element of collaboration. They could also be thought of as codifying students' natural impulse to find things out and to make sense of the world (Laevers 2000, Goswami 2008).

Table 2.2 gives some more details about each skill. You could use this list or amend it or draw up your own, but most lists will contain these elements somewhere or the other. These skills are referred to as *key skills* throughout the remainder of this book. Although this is slightly confusing with the OCR Key Skills, the term 'key skills' is widely used through the world in the way it is used in this book.

There is nothing sacrosanct about this list, and many countries and individual schools work successfully from different lists, but the above five elements do tend to occur widely. The reason why different lists can work equally successfully is that each skill is not discrete anyway, nor can the skills be taught or learned discretely. That is why, when attempts are made to break down the process into discrete elements, there will be disagreements about what the elements are, or where one starts and another ends. (The Rose Review in England used this list and then shortened it to four elements by subsuming 'analyse and synthesize' into 'investigate'.)

Many countries include 'problem solving' and 'critical thinking' in their list, while other countries see these as the result of all the others. (To solve a problem, you need to investigate, analyse and synthesize the information, create and develop different solutions, and evaluate your solutions. Critical thinking involves investigation, analysis, synthesis and evaluation, too.)

Table 2.2 Key skills

Key Skills (Thinking and Learning Skills)	
Investigate	Ask relevant questions, identify problems and question assumptions. Make observations, compare and contrast. Collect relevant information in a systematic way.
Analyse and synthesize	Analyse data collected to identify patterns and relationships. Synthesize information to make generalizations.
Create and develop ideas	Use imagination to explore possibilities and generate ideas. Suggest and try out innovative alternatives and find solutions to problems. Make reasoned decisions. Combine a range of approaches to find alternative solutions.
Evaluate	Develop effective criteria for judging effectiveness. Suggest improvements, modify and refine processes and outcomes, and analyse effectiveness in relation to intention. Ensure the practicality of ideas and developments.
Communicate	Communicate with a range of audiences, using and combining a range of media in ways appropriate to the audience and subject.

What is important in curriculum design is to be aware of the importance of a set of thinking and learning skills within and across the subject areas, and to build these into the curriculum.

These five skills can be seen as a common process of thinking and learning that is applied across the areas of learning. Listing them separately does not mean that they exist in isolation one from another; they are usually deployed and developed in concert. The line between the elements is often blurred; for example, analysis and synthesis could well be seen as part of investigating as it would be hard to do the one without the other. For example, students who wanted to make a wild life pond in the school grounds would investigate by finding out what lived in an existing pond nearby, analyse by distinguishing the different types, synthesize by sorting them into groups (plants and animals or fish, insects and crustaceans, etc.), create and develop by producing their own pond designs, evaluate by checking that these would actually work, and then communicate their ideas by drawings and plans. As far as the students are concerned, it is one seamless process. The holistic nature of this learning is recognized by academics as well as students (Gardner 1999, Perkins 2005, Goswami & Bryant 2007).

Essential literacy, numeracy and ICT: Back to basics!

Schools must ensure that students learn certain basic skills of literacy and numeracy. These take time to acquire, but lie at the heart of all other learning. They unlock learning in other areas, and allow young people to operate effectively in their lives. This is no less true in the twenty-first century than it was in the twentieth, although the emphasis has changed, the contexts in which the skills are applied are much wider, and the range of skills itself is now more extensive. The old nineteenth and twentieth century 'basics' are not sufficient for the twenty-first century. There still are some 'basics' that every student needs to learn, but they are not the same ones. The world has moved on.

This is reflected across the world where countries now identify these skills separately from the subjects. This is seen in different forms, such as 'civic literacy' and 'ICT' in Singapore and 'using languages, symbols and texts' in New Zealand. We have already referred to 'essential' or 'functional' literacy, numeracy and ICT in the English context.

These 'essential' or 'functional' aspects are really *competencies* rather than skills, because to operate effectively they require a certain amount of knowledge and understanding as well as skill. To be fully effective, the learner also needs the appropriate attitudes and dispositions. This combination is a competency.

Newspapers and some politicians in England are often urging schools to 'get back to basics'. By that they mean a focus on what used to be referred to as the 'Three Rs' of 'reading, writing and arithmetic' (obviously, spelling was not a strong point in those days). They were certainly the key skills for 1905, but the twenty-first century is making different demands. The range of communication is now much wider altogether. There was no demand for

ICT skills in 1905, but they have now become essential. The range of mathematics commonly demanded is also wider than the simple arithmetic that was sufficient in 1905.

It could therefore be argued that what we need is no longer the 'Three Rs' of 'reading, writing and arithmetic', but the '3Cs' of 'communication, calculation and computer competence'. (You may point out that this neat name doesn't really work because essential numeracy is wider than calculation, and ICT is more than computers – however, it is much neater if they all start with 'C'. There is good precedent for taking such liberties – neither writing nor arithmetic starts with 'R'! So, let's stick with the '3Cs'.)

The 3Cs

There will always be disagreements about what should be in, and what should be out, of any sort of list of this kind, but the identification of essential basic elements is an important aspect of curriculum design. If we remember Sinek's 'Why', it will be helpful to us. The reason we are equipping students with these 3Cs is to help them navigate their voyage of discovery through life. This should be our touchstone. 'How' we do that is by helping them develop key skills and competencies. 'What' these key skills and competencies are becomes much clearer when we remember 'Why' we are doing this at all.

Table 2.3 presents a list that is similar to the one in the Rose Review, and those of other countries. How does it measure up to that basic 'Why'? If students could do these things, would it help them explore the world and find their place in it with ease?

You may agree with the list in Table 2.3, or wish to amend or refine it. Many schools are finding it a useful starting point in identifying key aspects of learning that are essential in the twenty-first century. The list is reasonably up to date with its mention of digital media within literacy, but some schools have gone farther than this. The important, and helpful, point is to identify a range of access skills that can be built into a wide range of experiences.

The importance of identifying these 3Cs or essential elements of literacy, numeracy and ICT, is the way they then fit within curriculum design. If they are so important, do we allocate most of our time to these and then fit everything else in afterwards? Or is there a better way?

Table 2.3 The 3C competencies

Communication	Calculation	Computer competency
Listen attentively, talk clearly and confidently about their thoughts, opinions and ideas, listening carefully to others so that they can refine their thinking and express themselves effectively. *Read accurately and fluently to comprehend and critically respond* to texts of all kinds, on paper and on screen, in order to access ideas and information. *Write, present and broadcast* a range of ideas in a variety of forms for a range of audiences and purposes; communicate ideas accurately on paper, on screen and through multimodal texts. *Analyse, evaluate and criticize* a range of language to draw out meaning, purpose and effect.	*Represent and model situations* using a range of tools and applying logic and reasoning in order to predict, plan and try out options. *Use numbers* and *measurement* for accurate calculation, understanding of scale and make reasonable estimates. *Interpret and interrogate mathematical data* in graphs, spreadsheets and diagrams in order to draw inferences, recognise patterns and trends and assess likelihood. *Justify and support decisions and proposals,* communicating accurately using maths language, symbols and diagrams.	Find and select *information* from digital and online sources. *Create, manipulate and process information* using technology to capture and organize data, investigate patterns, explore options; combine still and moving images, sounds and texts to create multimedia products. *Collaborate, communicate and share* information using connectivity to work with and present to people and audiences within and beyond the school. *Refine and improve their work* make full use of the nature and pliability of digital information to explore options and improve outcomes.

The Michelin starred restaurant

If you can remember the beginning of this chapter, you might, of course, want to suggest that a posh restaurant is not particularly twenty-first century. (Unless, of course, it's run by Heston Blumenthal!) But successful restaurants have kept very much up to date. Not only are the kitchens very high tech, the menus, amount of food needed and budgets are worked out on spreadsheets. Website publicity and booking are essential. Menus need to be designed and advertising arranged. People's expectations of food and service have also changed over time.

To run the restaurant, students have to call on all of the 3Cs – communicating with the customers, suppliers and other team members; calculating menus, budgets and organizational schedules; computing the budget and ingredients on spreadsheets, printing the menus and publicity and updating the website.

It is also an interesting illustration of subjects within the curriculum. The amount of learning involved in running the restaurant involves a whole range of subjects: food technology, maths, science, ICT, English. But none of these appears as a separate subject when they are used. As soon as the subjects are applied in life, they begin to lose their boundaries.

The restaurant also contributed to students' personal development, social and negotiating skills. Just think how many of the 3Cs and the four UNESCO key competencies are integrally involved in running a restaurant: communication, collaboration, critical thinking and creativity, calculation and computer competence (how many more 'Cs' could you get?). Cooking and serving might seem to be 'old tech', but the competencies developed by the students are truly twenty-first century.

The next chapter of this book will look at how personal development, key skills and 3Cs can fit in with the subjects or disciplines to create rich learning for students.

3

A framework for the curriculum

The Olympic Games

Teams are working tirelessly to put together a bid to the Olympic Committee for the Games to come to the United Kingdom. They are designing stadia, planning transport infrastructure, carrying out environmental impact studies for the necessary buildings, preparing the benefit, impacts and sustainability statements, generating publicity material, shooting the promotional video and putting the whole bid together within the budget.

The teams are, of course, students and the bid is for their own town, not London. Each team is made up of students from Years 7, 8 and 9, and they meet each Friday for the whole day to work on the bids. The project started off with a visit from some famous Olympic athletes, and by watching some of the promotional videos and looking at extracts from some of the actual bids. The athletes are going to return at the end of term to judge the best bid. So they have ten Fridays for the work.

During this term, the normal timetable runs from Monday to Thursday, but all the lessons are focused on the bid. Maths is about the budget, geography and science, about the transport, sustainability and environmental impact, ICT and English, about the publicity and video, PE about games requirements, etc. The normal programmes have been adapted to focus on this theme. The same ground will be covered during Key Stage 3, but in a different order and with a different emphasis.

When the teams come together on Fridays, because team members come from three year groups, they have been to different lessons from Monday to Thursday, and so have something different to offer to the team. Year 7s have some expertise that

Year 9s lack. They plan their own work, including site visits, and allocate tasks within the group.

A further feature is that each team has a budget for buying teacher advice on Fridays. This really focuses the students' minds, and makes them particularly demanding. No time is to be wasted with off-task talk or vague advice: that would be a waste of money. They are also driven by the time constraint. Ten days get to look awfully short as the work progresses. Many teams stay after school through the week. Some get together at weekends. The bid becomes all-consuming.

It is all very well to talk about the 'lofty aims' for the curriculum in Chapter 1, and then add lists of skills, competencies and personal development in Chapter 2. But, how do all these elements come together along with the subject areas to provide a coherent curriculum for young people? How do lofty aspirations impact on the curriculum of a secondary school? What difference do they make to what Year 8 will be doing on a Thursday afternoon? If they do not impact on what actually goes on, then they will remain lofty aspirations and nothing more.

What many other countries have done is to create Curriculum Frameworks that provide a structure that shows how all the elements can come together to impact on learning. This is often done by establishing some key principles and values that need to underpin the whole curriculum, and then identifying the key skills and competencies that run right across it. This, in itself, is still theoretical and 'words on paper', but we need to follow this through to see how it impacts on curriculum design and so on the students themselves.

Singapore has a set of desired outcomes and principles that provide a setting for the competencies, which are presented in Figure 3.1.

Singapore				
	Desired outcomes	Principles	Social and emotional competencies	21st century competencies
	• Confident person • Self-directed learner • Active contributor • Concerned citizen	• Flexibility and diversity • Broad-based holistic education • Teach less–learn more	• Self-awareness • Self-management • Social awareness • Relationship management • Responsible decision making	• Civic literacy • Global awareness • Cross-curricular skills • Critical and media skills • Information and communication skills

Figure 3.1 Singapore's curriculum framework

New Zealand		
Principles	Values	Key competencies
 • High expectations • Treat of Waitangi • Cultural diversity • Inclusion • Learning to learn • Community engagement • Coherence • Future focus	• Excellence • Innovation, inquiry and curiosity • Diversity • Equity • Community participation • Ecological sustainability • Integrity • Respect	• Thinking • Using languages, symbols and texts • Managing self • Relating to others

Figure 3.2 New Zealand's curriculum framework

New Zealand has a framework of principles, values and key competencies, which are shown in Figure 3.2.

Does England have a curriculum framework?

The national curriculum for secondary schools in England has been put together in a piecemeal fashion since 1989. It started off as a set of subjects for which there were programmes of study and attainment targets. The functional skills were introduced in their final form in 2007, and the three aims were added in 2009 along with the PLTS. The framework would therefore look like the one in Figure 3.3.

The issue in England is that the framework has never been set out as such (have you ever seen that table before?), nor has any overall model been widely propagated that shows how this framework is supposed to impact

England		
Aims	PLTS	Functional skills
 • Successful learners • Confident individuals • Responsible citizens	• Independent enquirers • Effective participants • Reflective learners • Team workers • Self managers • Creative thinkers	• Literacy • Numeracy • ICT

Figure 3.3 England's curriculum framework

on the subjects and so influence curriculum design. The reality is that the framework was 'retrofitted' after the subject programmes had been set out, so was never incorporated properly. The issue is that it doesn't really work as a framework anyway, because it does not provide a model of how the different elements fit together.

A curriculum model

Singapore has set its competencies within a clear framework of outcomes and values. Figure 3.4 illustrates the centrality of the competencies, but does not show precisely how they fit with the subject areas that are also a requirement of the Singapore curriculum. A further diagram, or model, Figure 3.5, shows how the competencies are set in the context of the subject areas. There are two sets of central competencies: Life Skills and Knowledge Skills (it may be the translation, but the terms 'skills' and 'competency' are not always used consistently in these models). Life skills are broadly to do with personal development, health and well-being, and the knowledge skills are the 'key skills' or 'thinking and learning skills'. The subject areas are

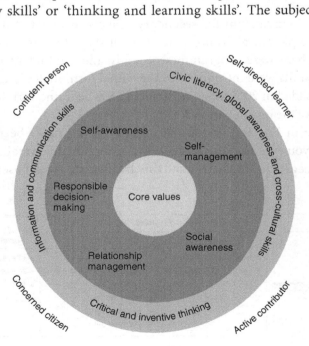

Figure 3.4 The Singapore core (Source: www.moe.gov.sg)

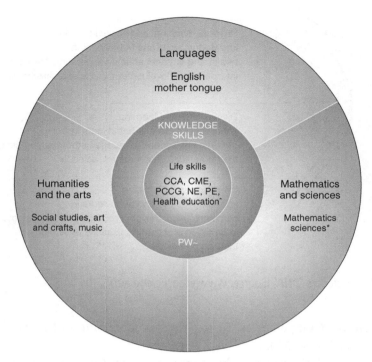

Figure 3.5 Singapore's curriculum framework (Source: www.moe.gov.sg)

grouped into three broad domains, and the skills are shown at the heart of the curriculum:

In this framework, PE is seen as an aspect of life skills rather than as a subject. Essential elements of literacy, numeracy and ICT (the 3Cs) are part of knowledge skills. The model illustrates the way the skills make an impact right across the subject areas, and are central to the curriculum.

The State of Victoria in Australia has a third 'strand' to its curriculum that it calls 'inter-disciplinary learning'. This is similar to the cross-curricular elements required in Finland and elsewhere, where students are required to engage in thematic studies that join subjects together. The Victoria model sees the three strands interweaving rather like a triple helix of DNA (see Figure 3.6).

It is envisaged that learning experiences are designed to combine these three elements, and we shall look closer at this in the next chapter.

A more generic model of how all these things fit together shows how the elements of aims, values, subject areas and what we might call

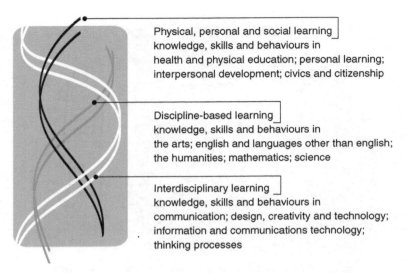

Physical, personal and social learning
knowledge, skills and behaviours in
health and physical education; personal learning;
interpersonal development; civics and citizenship

Discipline-based learning
knowledge, skills and behaviours in
the arts; english and languages other than english;
the humanities; mathematics; science

Interdisciplinary learning
knowledge, skills and behaviours in
communication; design, creativity and technology;
information and communications technology;
thinking processes

Figure 3.6 Victoria's 'DNA' (Source: www.vcaa.vic.edu.au/)

'21st Century Competencies' fit together to contribute to the whole curriculum (see Figure 3.7).

In this model, the values, subject areas and '21st Century Competencies' all come together to create the curriculum. And if the curriculum is successful, then it will achieve its ends and young people will develop into lifelong learners, critical thinkers and confident individuals (or whatever aims you have set).

It may seem odd to put the aims at the end in this way. Don't we start from the aims? In terms of design, we do start with the aims, but they should also be the outcome of the curriculum and the measure of its success.

Impact in the classroom

We could also look at the impact another way (Figure 3.8) with the subject areas and the three elements of the competencies contributing to the experiences of the secondary curriculum that we looked at in Chapter 1.

In the process of design, the curriculum designer draws upon the four elements to construct the wide range of learning experiences that students enjoy in school (see Figure 3.9).

The curriculum designer uses the four elements to construct the learning experiences, but the student sees it the other way round. From the student's

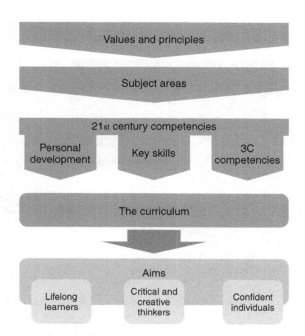

Figure 3.7 The overall framework

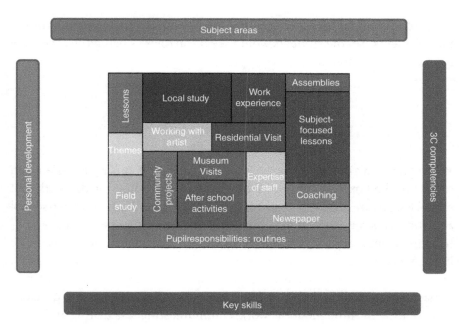

Figure 3.8 The impact

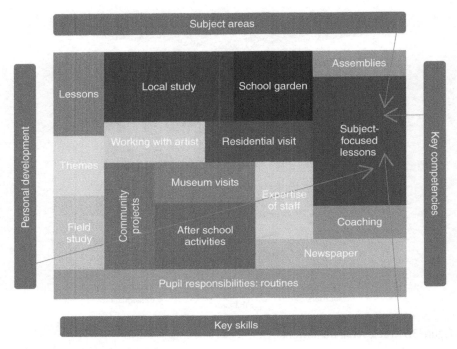

Figure 3.9 The impact on lessons

point of view, it is the experience that contributes to their learning in the four elements. So, the students would see the arrows as being the other way round. There is more of this in Chapter 9.

Olympian standards

When you think of the Olympic Games example, this was an experience in several of the boxes. The 'themes' box is a major location for the work, but school lessons are involved, as are visits, coaching, local study and after-school activities. When we look at the four outside elements, there was a major contribution from every subject area (every subject contributed, there was music in the video and translations for French and German visitors). There was a great contribution to personal development in terms of teamwork, confidence, initiative, resilience and adaptability. There was significant use and development of the 3Cs throughout the work: communicating, calculating and using computers. And all of the key skills were necessary to make the bid a success.

Rich experiences like this have no difficulty in making contributions to a wide range of learning. The trick is to recognize the extent of the learning going on, and then to build on it. An effective framework helps us take account of this richness.

And what if my country does not have one of the clear frameworks described above?

Some schools would be delighted to have the opportunity to draw up their own framework, and would relish the task of constructing one. Other schools may think that a framework like Singapore's looks pretty good and could be adapted to cooler climates. Or you may like to make use of the one in Figure 3.7. The key is to take the learning you intend for the students in your school and think through how it all fits together. Is there any direct way in which your school's aims can make an impact each time a learning experience is designed? What about students' personal development? Is this taken into account when learning is designed? What about the range of skills and competencies that we have been talking about?

Can all these things really impact directly on learning in the classroom? Can they really affect what Year 8 will be doing next Thursday afternoon?

Yes they can. And the secret of how they do it is a tree.

SECTION II

How do we organize learning?

4

The curriculum tree

Life's a Beach

Year 8 are on the beach building sandcastles, but it is winter and they are in the role of scientists and geographers rather than holidaymakers in this joint project. They are working in teams to answer a set of questions, almost all of which they have posed themselves. Why is the cliff higher at one end than the other? Why is the sand a different colour in places? Why is it higher one side of the groyne than the other? What is happening to the beach either side of the harbour breakwater? Why are those enormous concrete blocks below the cliffs? Why is there grass on the cliff but not on the lower land behind the beach?

To answer these questions, the students will have to come up with suggestions and devise methods of investigation. 'I think that the sand is higher because the sea washes it there'. 'But, why that side and not the other?' 'It's the same with the breakwater'. 'Perhaps the sea, sort of, slips sideways'. 'But how could we prove that?' They work in teams to plan ways of finding out the answers to these and other questions.

Having planned their investigations, they do, indeed, build sandcastles and watch the impact of the sea as it washes them away. But in their present role, they film the erosion in action, and time and measure the impact at various points along the beach.

They measure the drift of the sea with floats and stopwatches, check the types of pebbles at different points and work out how far they must have travelled. They track the movement of grains of sand, and film the water swirling around the concrete breakwaters to compare it to the river flow.

It occurred to them at one point in the afternoon that the cliff and beach are not just being 'washed away', but grains of sand and pieces of rock are being moved from one place to another. 'It doesn't disappear – it is just taken somewhere else! The whole shape of the landscape is changing'.

'If people hadn't built the groyne, the whole beach would get washed away'. 'And if they hadn't built the breakwater there would be nowhere to keep the fishing boats'. 'And those blocks are stopping the whole village being washed away'.

'Eureka' as someone else once said.

The question from the first chapter was 'How do the wider aims, values, skills and competencies impact on the subjects?' How do we design a curriculum that enables students to acquire the skills, competencies, attitudes and values that they might need to face the twenty-first century, and also be inducted into the major subject areas that they also need in order to face that century? Are the two compatible? Do we have to make a choice, or compromise on one to achieve the other? And can we, at the same time, make learning exciting, engaging and challenging?

One way of approaching this issue is to think of the curriculum as being a tree. In this tree we have 'branches of learning': science, the arts, humanities, etc. These branches themselves branch out into smaller ones. Science branches into physics, chemistry and biology. Humanities branches into history, geography and citizenship, etc. This is just a way of thinking about the curriculum and seeing the connections (see Figure 4.1).

At the end of the smaller branches (or twigs!) we find the leaves. The leaves are the individual bits of learning that are required by the national curriculum or by the syllabus or course. So, if we go up the humanities branch, and fork off along history, we shall find the Middle Ages, French Revolution or First World War. If we go up the science branch and then along physics, we get to 'electricity and magnetism' and 'forces'.

Most of our curriculum planning consists of arranging these leaves. Most of the thought that goes into reviewing a national curriculum is about what leaves we should have and what should be on them. In some cases, people look at the branches themselves and wonder if we need them at all – or whether we need extra ones. Look at the lowest branch on the right that

Figure 4.1 The branches of learning

seems to have been chopped off. What do you think that would have been?
Philosophy? Sociology?

Yet for all the time we spend thinking about the leaves, the model is
incomplete. There's a bit under the ground. A bit we never see and so seldom
think about. The bit that holds up all the rest and keeps it alive. The curriculum lacks roots.

Surely, the roots are where students learn to be critical thinkers and problem solvers, where they learn to work together in teams, develop their creativity and their social skills, learn to investigate, to evaluate, to develop new
ideas, to be enterprising and to communicate in a wide range of ways with a
wide range of people. They also develop personally as confident individuals,
willing to take risks, trying different methods and approaches, learning to

Figure 4.2 The whole curriculum

deal with setbacks and difficulties. The roots are where students develop those additional key skills and 3Cs that we discussed in Chapter 2.

Looking at the curriculum in the context of the model in Figure 4.2, we begin to see how subjects and wider competencies, attitudes and dispositions can fit together. We also see that it is unnecessary to debate whether the curriculum should only be about subjects, or whether subjects are more important than skills. The tree needs both. The roots cannot develop without the photosynthesis in the leaves, and the leaves cannot grow without the moisture from the roots. They need each other.

Each of the skills, competencies, attitudes and dispositions at the root of learning needs the context of a leaf to develop. Students cannot learn to solve problems unless they have some problems to solve – and those problems occur within the contexts of history, geography, science or technology or any other of the leaves. Students cannot learn to investigate unless they have something to investigate, and, again, the opportunities for investigation occur within the leaves. Students cannot learn to work together in teams unless the team has some enterprise in which to engage. None of the skills can be learned in a vacuum, and the subject disciplines, the established areas of human endeavour, mean that no such vacuum needs to exist.

This is not to say that the subject disciplines exist only to provide a context for the development of skills and competencies. They are important in their own right as knowledge frameworks and as ways of understanding the world. They are an essential part of being prepared for the twenty-first century. What the tree analogy makes clear is the symbiotic relationship between subject disciplines and skills. The skills cannot be developed without the context of the subject disciplines, and the possession of the skills is what enables learners to access the subject disciplines.

The root of the problem

Interestingly, to pursue the analogy, an individual leaf is not always critical to the tree's health. A leaf could fall off, and the tree can grow a new one. In fact, all the leaves could fall off and if the tree has good roots it can grow a whole new set of leaves. This process could be repeated year after year – and wouldn't this be called 'lifelong learning'? So isn't it the roots that promote lifelong learning? The roots are the skills and competencies that enable young people to continue learning, but also the attitudes and values that make them want to do so.

We can send a young person out into the world at 16 with a wonderful set of leaves, but if the roots are poorly developed, or if they have become 'pot-bound' because the curriculum has not allowed them to develop, then the young person has no grounding. At the first buffet of a twenty-first century wind, that tree will blow over and the young person will become Not in Education, Employment or Training (NEET). What will sustain them through life are good roots.

Yet not only do we spend most of our time thinking about the leaves, and rearranging them and arguing about whether one leaf is more important than another, we also test students in terms of the leaves; and when the inspectors call, they also spend their time looking at the leaves. But when we asked people what they thought young people needed to equip them for the twenty-first century, they answered in terms of roots.

Harvard University once ran an experiment over several years in which they invited a representative sample of graduates to retake their final examination a year later. Over 75 per cent failed. So we might conclude that there is little point in going to Harvard because a year later you will have forgotten everything you learned. But, of course, after three years at Harvard you are a different person: in terms of self-confidence, critical thinking, analysis and research skills, debate and discussion, explaining things, solving problems – in fact, all the roots. Yet it is not the roots that are tested. Of course, the graduates are much more proficient in their own subjects as well – but not always enough to pass their finals again!

There was an old saying that, 'Education is what remains after you've forgotten all they taught you'. What remains, of course, are the roots.

And some fell on stony ground

At this point, some people will be saying, I accept the analysis – but it's not fair. In my school we are trying to lay down roots in particularly stony ground. Up the road, in the leafy suburb, it's really easy for the students to grow roots; in fact, they come to school in Year 7 with their roots already well developed.

And this is true; which gives more weight to the model. Some students do come to school already able to co-operate and communicate, able to think critically to some extent and able to find out about things. They are curious and confident and can find things out for themselves. So no wonder they find it easy to learn. Yet, when students do not find it easy to learn, we do not always look to the roots as the reason; we more frequently concentrate on the leaves.

But it could well be that the very reason these young people are finding it hard to learn is that their 'roots' are not yet well established. Because they are not yet very good at co-operating, communicating, investigating, thinking critically or solving problems, and because they lack confidence to work independently, they find learning difficult. The leaves are failing to flourish because the roots are not well formed.

Once we start to look at the curriculum in this way, other things begin to fall into place. Not least the issue of curriculum design.

Looking at the trunk: The quality of students' learning experiences

What joins a tree's leaves to its roots is the trunk. In educational terms, the trunk is the quality of students' learning experiences. Some learning experiences are 'sterile', in that students gain a lot of knowledge about a 'leaf', but the experience does nothing to help them develop stronger roots. Other experiences are 'rich', in that they enable students to develop their understanding within a subject discipline, but also enable them to deepen and extend their roots as well.

In the example at the beginning of this chapter, students in Year 8 were learning about erosion, thus fulfilling a requirement of the English National Curriculum. In some schools this might have been a matter of reading textbook examples and making notes. But here, the learning experience described goes beyond that. The students were learning about erosion, but at the same time they were developing their skills of solving problems, thinking critically (is the drift of the sea really the reason for the sand being higher?), planning investigations and working together in teams. Working in this way also helped them develop self-confidence and an ability to work independently.

But did this skill development detract from their learning about erosion? If we examine their learning of geography in terms of the requirements existing at that time, we see that it was quite considerable.

- In terms of geographical and scientific information, they found out about the movement of the sea and a river and how this impacts on the surrounding landscape, and how human and physical processes can combine to shape an environment.

- In terms of geographic and scientific skills, they identified questions, planned an investigation, and they collected, analysed and evaluated evidence.

- Critically, they developed an understanding of the key concept – that the landscape we see is constantly changing and is the result of certain forces acting upon it.

They did well in terms of the English National Curriculum Levels of Attainment. In this system, Level 5 requires students to 'describe how

physical and human processes can lead to similarities and differences';
Level 6 requires 'understanding of the ways in which physical and human
processes lead to change in places'; and Level 7 requires students to 'explain
how interactions between physical and human processes change places and
environments'.

The very design of this learning experience ensured that the students
were working in the area of Level 6, because they were investigating a landscape where both human and physical processes were causing change. Their
investigations revealed the interplay between these factors, which then took
them to Level 7. The levels illustrated here are those of the English National
Curriculum, but within any national system this represents progress in
terms of geographical understanding. The process can be adapted to any
system.

The learning experience is rich because the roots of investigation, critical thinking and problem solving nourish the learning about erosion. At
the same time, the study of this aspect of human and physical processes
provides the context in which the 'roots' can develop. The 'trunk' of a rich
learning experience brings the two together.

Is this the curriculum or teaching?

Some people might well wish to suggest that the beach example is a matter
of a particular teaching and learning approach, not a different curriculum.
They are, of course, right in that the impact hinges around the approach,
but in the definition of the curriculum set out in Chapter 1, we said, 'All
the learning experiences the students receive as they go through school'.
By this definition, if you change the learning experience, you change the
curriculum.

This is more than just playing with words. The Year 8 students in question could have completed their geography topic by reading a textbook and
completing a worksheet. They would have been complying (to a certain
extent) with the national curriculum requirement to study erosion, but
their learning experience would have been very different from the pupils
carrying out their own investigations on the beach, who were also complying with the national curriculum by studying erosion. As a result of the
different learning experiences, the two sets of students will have learned
different things. Not least, in terms of learning key skills. But also the

geography they would have learned would be different, even if it all fell under the heading of 'erosion'. And if what they learn is different, then the curriculum is different.

Thus, the curriculum and the nature of teaching and learning are inextricably linked. You cannot change the one without changing the other. So there is a law of reciprocity here. A set of experiences (curriculum) that involves students working in co-operation, solving problems and finding things out will require different teaching and learning approaches from a set of learning experiences (curriculum) that involves students remembering facts and writing individually. And vice versa; different teaching and learning approaches will inevitably change the nature of the learning experiences, thereby changing the curriculum.

If we change the learning experiences, we change the curriculum. So if we want to change the curriculum, we need to change the very nature of the students' learning experiences.

How does this work at the design stage?

You can see the impact of this in the classroom, but how does it impact at the point of curriculum design?

One way of thinking about this is to see the two parts of the curriculum we have been talking about – subject disciplines (leaves) and a range of personal development skills, key skills and 3Cs (roots) – as forming a matrix. We can start the matrix with the subjects (Figure 4.3). (Before you ask what's happened to a modern foreign language (MFL), ICT and design and technology (D&T) – the diagram looked too crowded with them all in. They should be all there and they are all important!)

We can then add the key skills that we see as important, or relevant, to the particular group of students for whom we are designing these experiences. In the process of curriculum design, a school or a teacher would consider those skills that the students in that particular class needed to develop (see Figure 4.4).

These are depicted as arrows because they run right through the curriculum and impact on all of the subject disciplines. Together they form the matrix (see Figure 4.5).

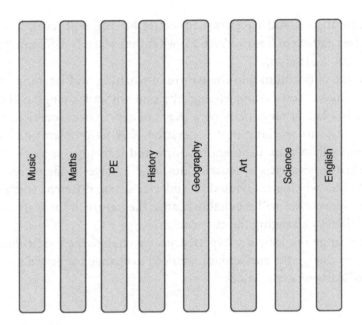

Figure 4.3 The subjects

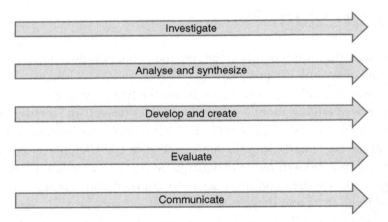

Figure 4.4 The key skills

The key point of this model is that the key skills run right through all the subject disciplines. Creativity does not just happen in art, and communication does not just happen in English. The focus becomes the intersections, and the crucial question now becomes, 'How can music help students develop their investigation skills?', and 'How can maths help them develop their

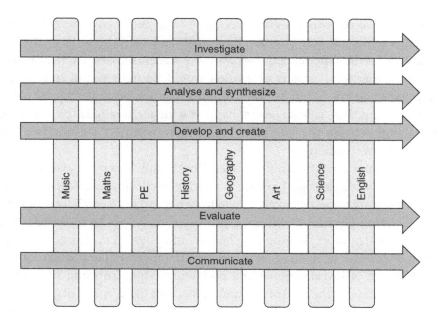

Figure 4.5 The matrix

creativity?' or 'How can geography help with communication?' Of course, there is no one-to-one match. Any subject discipline can help to develop any, or all, of the generic skills. It just depends on how learning is put together. This is where flexibility and variation come in. All schools might be studying erosion, but the focus within that study will vary with the particular generic skills being developed. This will depend upon the students concerned and could vary from year to year. One class might be good at investigations but not at communication, and so the focus would shift.

This need not be a matter of 'diluting' the learning within the subject disciplines in order to 'shoehorn' in the generic skills. Approaching the subject disciplines through skills actually enhances students' learning of the subjects. It is not a matter of having either one or the other. We can have both.

The matrix in action

The key to using the matrix within curriculum design is for schools and teachers to use both elements when designing sets of learning experiences. In the beach example, instead of setting out all the elements of erosion that could be covered within a given period of time and then arranging these elements into some sort of order, the teacher has used the skills as the key organizer for the experiences. If we want the students to develop their investigative skills, what aspects of erosion would be most useful to look at? Glaciers would not be too helpful to an investigation because they are painfully slow and there is none near at hand. But for a school near the coast, the interaction between the sea and human efforts to protect the land is a rich source of investigation.

The symbiotic relationship between 'roots' and 'leaves' is also seen in action at this design stage. In order to provide intellectual challenge to these Year 8 students, we would expect them to go beyond the Level 5 requirement of 'describing physical and human processes', and start to investigate the Level 6 element of 'explaining how human and physical processes interact'. The higher order demand of an interaction is a much richer context for the development of investigational and problem solving skills and so has the effect of increasing the level of demand. A focus on the 'content' of geography (the leaves) instead of the key skills is more likely to stick at the 'describing' of Level 5. As a result of their investigations and their wrestling with the problem, the students almost inevitably attained Level 7 because they could explain how the interaction was changing the local environment.

Far from diluting, or detracting from, the subject learning, the skills organizer has actually enhanced subject learning. In fact, a series of experiences like this could well bring the students to Level 8: 'Analyse the interactions within and between physical and human processes and show how these interactions can create diversity and help change places and environments'.

Design triangles

The tree and the matrix are good models for seeing how all the elements of a curriculum fit together, but they are not very useful as tools of curriculum design. A more useful model in this context is the triangulation of the leaves and two aspects of the roots: key skills and personal development. The process can be illustrated as in Figure 4.6.

In the example at the beginning of this chapter, the students were learning geography while developing their key skills of investigation, and also the personal development aspect of working together in teams. This could be illustrated as in Figure 4.7.

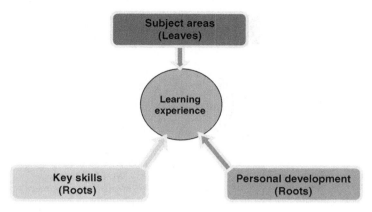

Figure 4.6 The design 'triangle'

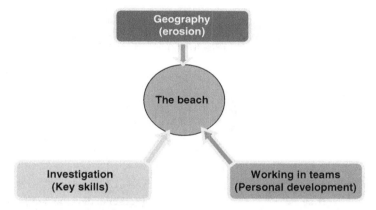

Figure 4.7 The investigation triangle

The model has been presented retrospectively here, but could be used as a design tool, listing the skills that need to be developed, and the context in which they need to be developed. This triangulation will define the sort of learning experience needed: one that addresses all three.

If the students in your class are already good at investigation, but need to develop their communication skills, and you still want to work within the same geographical context, then the learning experience would change. What do you think it could be? What would promote all three? The process would look as shown in Figure 4.8.

You might, for example, ask the students to set up a website to show how the physical and human forces were changing the environment. They would still be looking at erosion, still working in teams, but would need to think

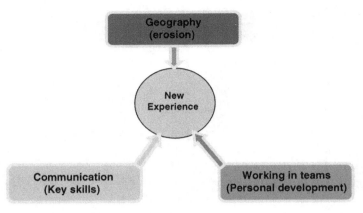

Figure 4.8 The communication triangle

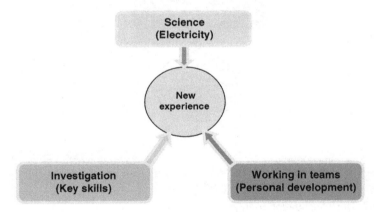

Figure 4.9 The electric triangle

about how they would communicate the information to others in writing, film, talk or an animation of some kind.

If we go back to the beach example, we could have kept the two skills the same, but changed the subject – perhaps investigating transport patterns instead of erosion, and again, another experience would be created.

This approach does not just work for history! How could we set these same skills in, say, science? What aspect of electricity would enable these skills to be developed? (see Figure 4.9).

There are any number of experiences here, depending on the aspect of science being studied; for example, students could be asked to work in teams to find as many ways as they could of varying the intensity of light coming from a bulb.

Making use of this approach

Curriculum planning meetings are often about making lists of all the things we want the students to learn. A curriculum design meeting would be about thinking up new experiences that would enable students to enhance their personal development and key skills in the context of subjects. In joining 'leaves' to 'roots' in this way, the 'trunk' of learning always seems to become more challenging, more meaningful and more exciting. Students enjoy their learning, and learn more. And when they learn more, guess what? They do better in tests! You really can't go wrong!

The design process

We have been looking at how key skills can be built into design at a general level, but need to look more closely within skills and at how they fit with and support knowledge and understanding. We have not included the 3Cs at this stage in order not to complicate the picture. But they must also be part of the design, and in Chapter 7 we will look at how these are part of the design structure.

At the time of writing this, the English National Curriculum is being reviewed and some of the elements we have been discussing may be removed. But people will always study erosion in geography, and whatever the new national curriculum says, it will be schools that interpret it into learning experiences for students. It will be schools that put the curriculum together in ways that are exciting and engaging; that connect with students' lives and yet open up possibilities they have not considered. These are the rich experiences that link leaves to roots and provide for the full intellectual development of the young person. This is the way in which we enable young people to explore their world and find their place in it.

These cultivate the deep roots of learning.

5

The deep roots of learning

Animating Turner

A group of Year 10 students were making an animated film, but were dissatisfied with the results. First, the movements looked all wrong. It wasn't that they were jerky, they could correct that with the number of frame shots; what it was, was that it didn't look at all real. When their characters jumped, they seemed to just fly up into the air in a quite unreal way. 'It just looks daft'. They tried jumping up and down themselves, but it all happens too quickly to work out how it looks. Then the thought struck, reverse the stop-frame technique!

They filmed themselves jumping and watched the film frame by frame to see how arms and legs combine in a jump. To make it easier, they drew a grid on the wall and filmed themselves moving against it. They then analysed the movements through the squares and made their characters move in just the same way. Problem solved.

But they were still not totally satisfied. They were familiar with Wallace and Gromit and could not understand why the professionally made animations looked so full and three dimensional and theirs looked flat. They were, after all, actually 3D in the first place. 'How do they do it?' 'Do they use more than one camera?' Back to *The Wrong Trousers*, stopping the film and scrutinizing it in detail.

Then the light dawned, quite literally. One of the group who was studying art as well, saw an echo of Turner's paintings in Wallace's house. 'It's the light!' A feature of Turner's painting is the way light seems to suffuse the whole scene. The student animators had been using just ordinary light for their animation, Aardman use clever backlights and angles to emphasize the shapes.

Back to the animation with lights and lamps tilted at all angles until it all comes to life.

If we recognize in the tree analogy that there are roots to learning as well as leaves of content that need to be covered, then we also have a model by which we can build them into curriculum design. This we can do even if the national curriculum were to change in a national review, and even if the new national curriculum seems to contain nothing but leaves. It will still be our responsibility as schools to ensure that our pupils receive a broad, balanced and rounded education that prepares them fully for the future. This is why the way we design the curriculum is so important.

There are two important points in the consideration of roots:

1. They are a significant part of learning and so should be a significant part of design.
2. Designing the curriculum this way deepens learning itself.

There is a notion of 'deep learning' that takes learning beyond superficial memorization to more complex understanding. This has been dealt with by writers from Piaget (1950) and Bruner (1966) to Hargreaves (2006), all of whom stress the need to take learning beyond the disconnected, superficial and transient, and let it become meaningful, deep and lasting.

Bloom's taxonomy

Many countries still use Bloom's 1956 *Taxonomy of Learning Objectives* in their approach to curriculum design. Bloom saw three levels of 'knowledge' that form a hierarchy. The simplest form of knowledge ('knowing that') is the recall of information. The second level ('knowing how to') is what we might usually see as skills; being able to do something. The highest level ('knowing about') is the grasp of universal concepts, theories and structures that lead to understanding.

Bloom suggested that within the cognitive domain, there is a hierarchy of processes. (This causes a directional conflict of the metaphors! We talk of 'deep learning', while Bloom talks of a rising scale of 'higher order' abilities. 'Higher'? or 'deeper'? These are just metaphors to refer to learning that goes beyond the superficial. Some people use the term 'profound learning'.)

Whether we use a metaphor such as 'higher' or 'deeper', or call it 'profound learning', the important thing is the order of the hierarchy, which Bloom suggests is (in ascending order) as in Figure 5.1.

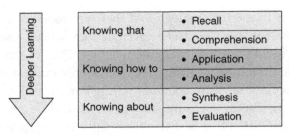

Figure 5.1 Deeper learning

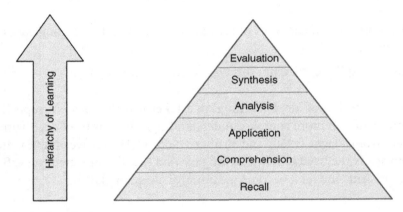

Figure 5.2 Bloom's taxonomy

Bloom suggests that the recall of information is the most superficial level and that deeper learning involves doing something with that information, until an overall understanding is reached. His taxonomy is usually presented as a triangle (see Figure 5.2).

Several people have sought to 'update' this taxonomy, and one update that is widely used is by one of Bloom's pupils, Lorin Anderson, in 2001. Anderson basically turned the nouns to verbs, merged analysis and synthesis and added creativity. The hierarchy then becomes:

Remembering, comprehending, applying, analysing, evaluating and creating.

In terms of the 'tree' model (Figure 5.3), the first two (remembering and comprehending) are the leaves, so it is the addition of the roots that 'deepens' the learning by moving it from the superficial to the higher-order level.

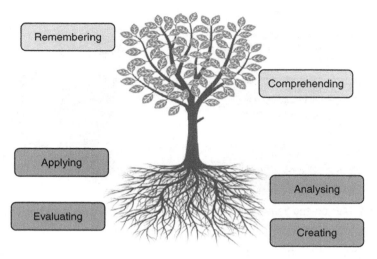

Figure 5.3 The tree in bloom

When students start to apply their comprehension, when they begin to analyse the information they have acquired, to evaluate its worth and to use the information creatively, it is then that they have taken it to the deeper (or higher!) level of full conceptual development. The term we usually use for this deep conceptual level is 'to understand'.

The implication of this analysis for curriculum design is that students need to be engaged with their learning at the levels of the application of skills for the learning to be deep. Lessons where students sit passively absorbing information will leave them at best at the level of comprehension. The deep learning that comes from the application of skills needs the active engagement of the learner. So we need to design experiences that give this opportunity.

Marton and Saljo

In 2008, Marton and Saljo of Gothenburg University considered 'Deep and Surface Approaches to Learning' and saw three levels, which they likened to coffee moving through the cafetiere to make the final brew. This is an interesting metaphor, because we often try to speed up the coffee process by trying to ram it down with the plunger – but when it is ready it sinks of its own accord. Then all you have to do is rest your finger on the plunger and it sinks gently. And you get much better coffee if you wait for it to have

- Memorising facts
- Learning to pass exams
- Learning detached from the real world

- Questioning
- Changing ways of thinking
- Engaging with learning

- Searching for meaning
- Approaching learning from the real world
- An holistic approach to learning

Figure 5.4 Marton and Saljo's three levels

infused properly! This might conjure up an image of unfortunate students having learning rammed down their throats, when the teacher would be better advised to give them time to absorb their learning and to let it sink in. The ramming down their throats will not make good learning anyway. In the example at the beginning of this chapter, the student animators were given time to find their own solution, and were all the better for it.

Marton and Saljo's three levels are shown in Figure 5.4.

Making it work in school

The notion of 'deep learning' was also addressed in a series of papers for the Specialist Schools and Academies Trust (SSAT) by David Hargreaves in 2006. Hargreaves argues that deep learning is brought about by the greater involvement of the learner in the process, so that they become active agents in their own learning rather than passive recipients of teaching. He sees this as the process of 'personalising' learning. In this analysis, to achieve deep learning, it is necessary to provide what Hargreaves calls:

- Deep experiences
- Deep support

This requires changes both in curriculum design and in the nature of teaching and learning to create the 'co-construction of learning'. This co-construction can be carried out between teacher and pupil, and

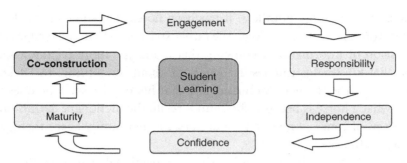

Figure 5.5 Hargreaves's co-construction

between pupil and pupil. Hargreaves sees a cycle around student learning (Figure 5.5).

Hargreaves' notion of 'co-construction' involves the active engagement of the learner. Learning moves from the passive to the active, and involves responsibility and independence as a route to maturity and co-construction.

Deep learning in action

The student animators were engaging in the co-construction of learning, and so, in Hargreaves's terms, deepening it. They were active, independent, responsible and engaged. In terms of Bloom's amended taxonomy, they were also operating at the highest (deepest!) level of creativity, having applied their learning, analysed and evaluated all they had found out about the appearance of the animation, and setting that in the context of other learning at school.

In fact, all the examples we have looked at so far (and will see in the following chapters) also go a long way down in terms of the roots, and so achieve deep learning.

The nature of knowledge

Seeing skills as the way in which knowledge and understanding are deepened makes the continuing debate about whether knowledge is more important than skills even more pointless. It has been noted that some of the debate comes from the contrast between the rather strict view that knowledge is the possession of information ('knowing that'), and the more common-sense view, that knowledge implies 'knowing all about' something. In Dickens' *Hard Times*, the teacher Gradgrind says that his pupil Sissy Jupe does not know what a horse is because she cannot recite the dictionary definition of one. Sissy, of course, knows all about horses as her family keeps them, and she looks after them.

This Dickensian divide is still driving educational debate in England. Presumably, no one would oppose the 'deep knowledge' that Sissy has of horses. And no one would advocate the superficial memorization of Gradgrind's 'facts'. Yet there seems to be a feeling among some non-educationalists that there is insufficient 'knowledge' in the English National Curriculum, or being taught in schools. This may be because there are few 'facts' listed in the national programmes of study. This is mainly because there are so many facts that a human being learns by the age of 16 that it is impossible to list them all. If we were to attempt to list all the things that Sissy knew about horses, the list would be immense. It would certainly exceed the pupil Bitzer's definition that so pleased Gradgrind: 'Quadruped. Graminivorous. Forty teeth, namely twenty-four grinders, four eye-teeth, and twelve incisors. Sheds coat in the spring; in marshy countries, sheds hoofs, too. Hoofs hard, but requiring to be shod with iron. Age known by marks in mouth'.

This is the reason that the national programmes of study so frequently use the phrase 'Pupils should be taught about . . .', rather than 'Pupils should be taught that . . .'. Learning 'about' something implies not only a wider range of knowledge, it also implies that the knowledge is sorted into some order. This moves the knowledge from Bloom's first to second stage, that of comprehension. It is impossible to prescribe every piece of information that a child should acquire. So specifying that students should 'learn about' certain things actually *increases* the amount of knowledge they will learn, as they will almost certainly learn more than could be prescribed. What is lost in this transaction, of course, is total control of the specific knowledge being acquired. It may well be this desire for control that is fuelling the debate about knowledge, whatever is being said about freedom and flexibility.

Sissy Jupe's knowledge about horses did not come from Gradgrind's lessons. It came from her first-hand experiences in practical situations that were relevant to her life: experiences in which she was guided by people who were important to her, and to whom she had emotional commitment. She was mixing skills with knowledge. She was applying her knowledge to looking after her horses and so had deepened her learning.

The third form of knowledge is 'knowing how' to do something. This always suggests a skill, rather than informational or conceptual knowledge, but it is part of common usage. There is even an element of uncertainty here: Is *knowing how* to do something the same as *being able* to do it? For example, you may know how to play darts: you have to stand on the line and throw the dart so that it sticks in the board. However, that does not mean that the dart will hit the board when you throw it, or stick in the board if it hits it. It certainly doesn't mean it will stick in the treble twenty. This meaning of 'knowing how' is not the same as 'being able to'.

There are many lessons that students are still being taught in a way that will enable them to answer questions, or even to do well in tests, but not to apply the things they are learning in practical situations. They can tell you how to play darts, but cannot throw a dart themselves. The students are stuck at the superficial level of Bloom's second stage.

It is only when knowledge becomes 'knowing about' and is acquired in the context of the application of skills that we will achieve deep learning. This needs an holistic approach.

An holistic approach

The analysis that sees skills as a way of deepening learning sees the skills as integral to the development of knowledge and understanding. There is often a question about whether skills should be taught separately, and then applied in context, or whether they should be learned in the context in which they will be applied. The answer to this, like the answer to many design questions, is: 'both', but depending on the context and learner.

The danger of teaching a skill in isolation from its context of use is three fold. The first point is that the student may not see the point of the skill in isolation and so fail to comprehend what the skill is for. In an adult context, it is pointless trying to teach someone how to finesse in the card game bridge before the player can see why you would ever need to do so. After you have lost your Queen to your opponents' King a few times even though you held the ace, you will fully understand what is going on and so be ready to learn the skill. The second point is that you will also be keen to learn the skill because you have gained some emotional commitment to learning. Finally, there is growing evidence that skills learned in context are much more likely to be able to be applied in context.

This is why we often give students the opportunity to explore new materials or talk about new situations before we start instruction. 'Have a go and see what you can do.' Or 'How do you think we could do this?' This gives the students some context in which they can understand the new learning; some pegs on which they can hang new ideas. Without this initial familiarity with a new context, new ideas and information are often meaningless. This is why students sometimes simply do not understand something, even though the explanation seems so clear. In technical terms, they do not have a mental 'schema' that allows them to accommodate the new information.

This is not to say that there will not be times when it will be necessary to teach a skill before experiencing the context of its application. Using a chainsaw is usually given as an example of learning where exploratory methods would be inappropriate. However, even here the new user will always have some idea about the context of cutting and using hand tools. There will also be times when we need to stop and think about why things are not going right. This is the time when the need for the skill becomes apparent, when the students understand the context, and will have a commitment to learning it. At this point, the skill is taught separately, but only because the context has already been fully established, and will be there ready for the skill to be practised immediately before the learning is lost.

Have you ever stood in a group around a computer while someone demonstrated some new program or technique? By the time you get to use the new program yourself, you always seem to have forgotten what they said. You need to use the new techniques straight away in order for them to become embedded.

Being embedded means the learning was deep.

The importance of knowledge

Discussions about the curriculum at a political level often become polarized into the false dichotomy that education is either about knowledge or about skills. This book is arguing that successful education cannot have the one without the other. The deployment of Bloom's skills that constitute the deeper aspects of learning such as synthesis and analysis cannot be done in a vacuum. There must be a knowledge base to the process. The ability to analyse and synthesize is based upon having sufficient knowledge to do so. It would not be possible to make a thorough analysis of a topic if one had only limited knowledge about it. Synthesizing is about putting together information from various sources and so implies the possession of a range of information. To achieve the pinnacle (or deepest level!) of Bloom's taxonomy – or Anderson's updated version, that of 'creating' – it would be necessary to make connections and interpretations that had not been made before, using the knowledge creatively. In Bloom's original terms, the highest level was 'evaluation', by which he meant the ability to evaluate the knowledge gained in terms of its reliability, validity and usefulness to the task in hand. To reach either pinnacle, it would be essential to have a wide range of knowledge and to have the ability to scan across it for similarities, differences and connections. Without the wide knowledge base, this depth of understanding cannot be reached.

But the two are reciprocal. It is by the application of the knowledge that understanding is deepened. It is not until knowledge is applied, analysed and synthesized that it is turned into understanding. It is the process of application and analysis that leads the learner to search for more examples and other cases. This turns the process into synthesis, which builds the need for even more knowledge. With sufficient knowledge, and the ability to apply that knowledge, comes the level of using it creatively.

The student animators were able to apply the knowledge they had gained in one area of learning to another in order to solve their problem, so could be seen as operating at the Anderson/Bloom 'creative' level. They could do this because they were not being taught theoretically, but had been placed in a practical situation and had been given the opportunity, in Hargreaves's terms, to 'co-construct' learning. Both roots and leaves are involved in this process, and it has brought them to a deep level of understanding.

Key concepts

There is a further way in which curriculum design can work within a subject, or across subjects, to deepen learning.

The curriculum can sometimes seem like an endless, and increasingly tedious, list of things to be learned. It can seem like this to teachers who wonder if they will ever manage to 'get through it all', and it can seem like this to students who not only have to get through it all, but also have to remember it all for a test. Seen this way, the whole point of learning a subject can be lost in a mass of detail. Students can end up with a great deal of remembered information, but they do not have a system of organizing that information in their minds. This often comes about from the way the curriculum is designed within the subject. If design starts with the list of things to be learned, the curriculum generally ends up being a list of things to be learned. However, if the starting point is the coherence of the subject over the three years of Key Stage 3, or all the secondary years, then it is possible to design learning from the point of view of its underlying structure.

This structure is usually found in the 'big ideas' or the 'key concepts' that lie behind the selection of information in the first place. These will be familiar to subject specialists, and in England they are the basis of the Level Descriptions that set out expectations within the attainment targets. For example, in geography a key concept is that the landscape we see has been shaped by physical forces over time, or that the way people live is affected by their physical environment.

Overall, we are talking about the 'big ideas' that have shaped human thought over the ages and which have brought us to our present levels of understanding. This may sound rather high-flown, but surely our young people should leave school with a grasp of these key ideas, rather than a collection of information that they will soon forget like the Harvard students.

By taking a set of these key concepts as our organizers, the 'content' of the curriculum can become more meaningful. For example, the students on the beach in Chapter 4 are focusing on erosion because they are developing the 'landscape' concept above. Had the curriculum been organized around the 'way people live' concept, then they would have been more interested in the fishing village at the end of the beach.

This approach can be illustrated with the same sort of 'design triangle' that we used for looking at how skills and the 3Cs fit with subjects. This time, the triangles illustrate how learning can be structured within a subject. The third point of the triangle in this model would be the specific subject skills (see Figure 5.6).

Subject skills

We have been talking so far about generic skills or competencies that apply across all subjects. But some skills are specific to a particular subject such as

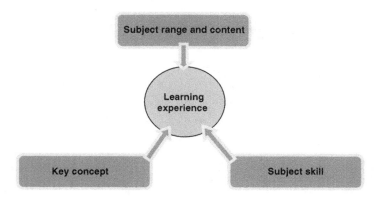

Figure 5.6 The subject triangle

carrying out a scientific investigation, or interpreting data in mathematics, or carrying out fieldwork in geography. Like the generic skills or competencies, these skills need to be part of the design of the curriculum, and so they form the third point of the triangle.

The role of curriculum design is to come up with a learning experience within the context of the range and content of the subject that will give students the opportunity to develop the needed skill while illustrating and clarifying the selected key concept. It is by putting these three together that learning experiences become richer and learning becomes deeper.

The model in Figure 5.6 shows how these three elements come together to structure the learning experience. The two elements of key concept and subject skill become 'organizers' of the subject 'range and content' – the list of things that need to be learned.

So the students on the beach were pursuing the key concept of landscapes being the result of physical forces, and the subject skill of carrying out fieldwork. In this example, 'erosion and deposition' is the element of the 'range and content' that has been chosen to illustrate the key concept and give opportunity to develop the subject skill (see Figure 5.7).

If we change one of the three elements, then the learning experience will need to be different. For example, if the students were already good at fieldwork and needed to improve their mapping skills, then even though the key concept remains 'landscape' and the element of the range and content remains 'erosion and deposition', the learning experience would need to be different. What would you suggest in this case? There are many alternatives, but one would be for the students to study maps of river and glacial valleys or different coastal areas to interpret what has happened to the

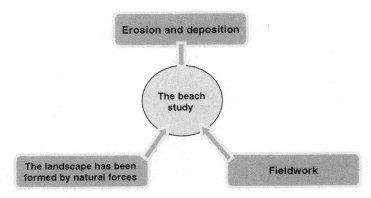

Figure 5.7 The beach triangle

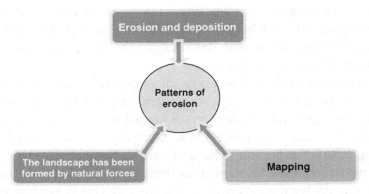

Figure 5.8 The erosion triangle

landscape to produce the valleys or the coves, cliffs and banks on the coast (see Figure 5.8).

Alternatively, if the subject skill was still fieldwork, but the key concept was the impact of human activity on the environment, then the learning activity would change again, and would focus on the way the harbour and sea defences impacted on erosion and deposition (see Figure 5.9).

The model of design in Figure 5.9 has implications for all subjects, and for the overall curriculum itself. As soon as the elements of key concepts and subject skills are taken account of in design, the nature of the learning experiences change. These experiences tend to become more active and give students more scope for independence. Learning experiences inevitably involve the application of the chosen skills, so immediately take learning deeper through Bloom's taxonomy. As we discussed in Chapter 2, the building of

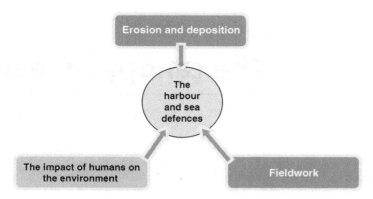

Figure 5.9 The harbour triangle

a concept involves more than the passing on of information, so this takes it even deeper.

As a result of this deeper learning, students are more likely to end up with an overall understanding that not only organizes the knowledge they have gained, but which also extends the amount of knowledge, while making it all easier to recall. All the ingredients they need to do well in tests and examinations!

So it is not necessary to choose between knowledge and skills because they need each other, and when developed together, both are stronger.

Across the subjects

Within a subject, this approach to design can be fairly straightforward and involves at most a re-sorting of the content already covered. There are, however, implications for the nature of teaching and learning and these in turn have implications for the timetable (few of the learning experiences in these examples occur within a one-hour lesson in a classroom). We shall be looking at these implications in Chapter 11.

There are also implications for the overall organization of the curriculum when we start to build in the generic key skills and the 3Cs that we discussed at the beginning of this chapter. That is what we shall be looking at next.

6 The canopy of leaves

> **Victorian Film-makers**
> Year 9 have made a film that shows the development of their town during the Victorian period. The film starts with an old map depicting a small village and the map grows showing streets and houses being added. Railways snake out to other towns. A river disappears as it is built over. Bridges appear over the larger river. The buildings become more densely packed and more extensive. A calendar clicks round in the top corner showing the passing of time.
>
> A series of photographs come and go showing the changing of fashions and the passing of time. The background music shows the development of a Victorian music hall, and the voiceover explains the economic reasons for such expansion.
>
> The DVD is on sale in school, in the local information office and around town. It raises money for the school, sparks interest in local history and raises the positive profile of the school.
>
> And, of course, some learning has gone on as well.

In Chapter 1, we spoke about our students needing to set out on their journey through life, while also taking account of the accumulated knowledge and experience of all those people who have gone before. That accumulated knowledge and experience has been stored and catalogued over the centuries. The systems of categorization and storage have varied through those centuries. Medieval universities in Europe studied medicine, law, theology and the liberal arts. Those liberal arts included: arithmetic, geometry, astronomy, music theory, grammar, logic and rhetoric.

Over the years, knowledge has grown and been constantly reclassified into different groups or subjects. These subjects, or 'subject disciplines', are more than stores of knowledge. They have created structures for understanding that knowledge, and have developed methodologies for accumulating new knowledge. These are systems of thought into which young people have a right to be inducted. In medieval times, an educated elite kept the masses in ignorance. Education is about the right of every human being to have access to learning. This is the role of the curriculum.

The Victorian film-makers were accessing knowledge as well as making a film. But what subject were they studying? We all know the answer to this question. The students were clearly engaged in many subjects at once, and we do not need to list them. The issue is whether subjects are helpful and essential disciplines, or whether they get in the way of the sort of organic and joined-up learning that happened while making the film in the example at the beginning of this chapter, or on the beach in Chapter 4. Is it better to mix subjects up like this or to study them separately?

In the analogy of a tree, there are branches of knowledge, and the twigs form the subjects. It is these branches and twigs that contain the leaves – the fragments of learning that hang together to form the canopy that makes sense, or not, to the learner. When we look back on our schooling, most people can remember a few remarkable lessons but, in the main, the lessons coalesce into an overall impression of the subjects and of schooling. We tend to view the canopy rather than the individual leaves. This overall view may, of course, be beneficial to our understanding of the world. Too much detail does not necessarily lead to a clearer picture. Hirsch (1988) refers to the 'vague knowledge' that he sees as forming the essential 'schemata' that structure our understandings.

The branches themselves are interesting. In certain subjects some people will feel their growth was stunted, in others they were able to blossom, and in yet others their growth was characterized by spurts and stops.

In relatively recent times, we have begun to question whether individuals are attracted to certain subjects or whether they have aptitudes in some but not others. Da Vinci might have excelled in science as well as the arts, but most do not. Or could it be to do with other factors? Maybe the teaching, the school organization, the students' expectations and backgrounds make the difference. Some of the variation could be due to the way we organize and present learning; how we let the canopy of learning emerge and flourish.

Should we organize learning into subjects?

It can be argued that the real world does not present itself in subjects and therefore learning about them should be holistic and natural, spontaneous and responsive. However, we have inherited a structure of learning and understanding that does use subject divisions, even if these are neither universally recognized around the world, nor related directly to the way in which that world works. However, we have had subjects for so long that it seems hard to step away from them. Universities use them and we examine them.

There is a need for young people to be 'inducted' into the subject disciplines because they are the major systems of human thought, and the ways in which society has stored its wisdom. But students also need to see the connections between one subject discipline and another. In order to understand the world fully and be able to operate effectively within it, they need to see its interconnectedness and realize that not only does one thing impact on another, but that looking at life through more than one lens enhances understanding.

Many countries take account of this double need in their national curriculum. Finland (Figure 6.1) and New Zealand (Figure 6.2) are among many to make specific reference to the need for integration.

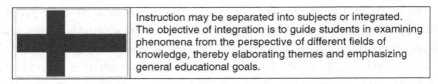

Instruction may be separated into subjects or integrated. The objective of integration is to guide students in examining phenomena from the perspective of different fields of knowledge, thereby elaborating themes and emphasizing general educational goals.

Figure 6.1 Finland

| While the learning areas are presented as distinct, this should not limit the ways in which schools structure the learning experiences offered to students. All learning should make use of the natural connections that exist between learning areas and that link learning areas to the values and key competencies. |

Figure 6.2 New Zealand

| • Growth as a person
• Cultural identity and internationalism
• Media skills and communication
• Participatory citizenship and entrepreneurship
• Responsibility for the environment, wellbeing and a sustainable future
• Safety and traffic
• Technology and the individual |

Figure 6.3 Finland's cross-curricular themes

English schools have the same freedom and flexibility. There is no statutory requirement to teach the curriculum as separate subjects. So we need to decide whether to or not, or whether to teach parts of subjects separately and some parts in connection with others. And we need to establish the grounds for making these decisions. To do this we need to look at the subjects themselves.

In some countries, cross-curricular themes are a required part of the national curriculum, so schools are required to spend at least some of their time teaching subjects through themes. It is interesting to note that some countries that do very well in international comparisons in terms of subjects, also require cross-curricular themes. For example, Finland sets out seven cross-curricular themes (Figure 6.3). In these themes, schools are required to integrate the contribution of a number of subjects in an holistic approach.

Of course, the English National Curriculum has the seven cross-curriculum dimensions:

1. Identity and cultural diversity

2. Healthy lifestyles

3. Community participation

4. Enterprise

5. Global dimension and sustainable development

6. Technology and the media

7. Creativity and critical thinking

Although introduced alongside the new English National Curriculum in 2008, the dimensions were never made a statutory part of it. Nor do they really provide the sort of themes around which different subjects can coalesce. However, many schools have adapted them successfully as vehicles for combining work across a number of subjects.

The list of subjects

In Chapter 2, we looked at the list of subjects that has been the English National Curriculum since 1989 and noted that the list had changed little from 1905. This gives the list an air of permanency and authenticity. But when we look in detail, it is not as fixed and permanent as it seems. Not all countries have the same list. Some countries include other subjects; for example, philosophy is compulsory in France, and most countries include a modern foreign language at primary level. Some countries omit some subjects on the English list, or arrange them in different ways; for example, many countries list 'social studies' rather than history and geography, and much of what is in geography in England is found in science in other countries (rocks, erosion, climate, etc.). Many countries have much broader areas of learning; see, for example, Figure 6.4.

New Zealand has broad categories such as 'The arts' and 'Social science'. Singapore lists 'Health education' and 'Physical education' separately, while New Zealand puts them together. In both cases, these lists are just ways of setting out broad entitlements for students and of defining a rounded curriculum. In neither country are schools required to arrange the curriculum in these ways.

What is a subject?

But what distinguishes one subject from another? Clearly there is no international agreement about this, nor have the subject boundaries stayed the

Singapore	New Zealand
Mother tongue	English
English	Other language
Maths	The arts
Civics and moral education	Health and physical education
Art and craft	Maths and statistics
Music	Science
Health education	Social science
Social studies	Technology
Physical education	
Science (From Grade 4)	

Figure 6.4 A range of subjects

same over time in any one country. We suggest that there are three key reasons why subject disciplines are important. They represent:

1. Bodies of accumulated knowledge
2. Structures for understanding that knowledge
3. Systems of finding new knowledge within those structures

These categories take us back to the three forms of learning in Chapter 1: knowledge, understanding and skills. These are the three aspects that distinguish one subject from another. It is not just the content of the knowledge (this often overlaps), it is also the way in which that knowledge is structured into understanding, and the methodologies used within the subject. Together, these are the 'disciplines'.

Many years ago, Peters (1971) suggested that what distinguished one subject from another was the way in which the truth of a proposition is established. For example, the truth of the proposition that 'metals expand when heated' can be established by a series of experiments within a scientific methodology. But the methods needed to establish that 'the invention of the bicycle was responsible for changing patterns of marriage', a different (historical) set again. Peters' logic brought him to eight subjects – and they were not the same as our English National Curriculum subjects.

There are many other practical or theoretical ways of arranging learning such as Phenix's *Realms of Meaning* (1964) or Anderson et al.'s *Taxonomy for Learning, Teaching and Assessing* (2001), which point to other groupings. This is why there is no international consensus about what the subjects are or should be, or where one ends and another begins. For example, in terms of the English National Curriculum, students looking in rock pools on the beach would be studying geography when they found out how the pools were formed, but science when they found out what lived inside them. In Singapore, they would be doing science all the time, because both life and the erosion of rocks are included in that subject. Does it matter? Is it not more important that students should be finding out about the world around them rather than argue about which piece of learning goes where?

Although there may be disagreement about where lines are drawn and what goes where, there is a wide consensus that what is important to a subject is more than the knowledge content. There are systems and structures of thought that define how we understand a subject area, there are the specific methodologies that are used within the subject, and there is the range of information that has been accumulated by people working within that subject.

In Chapter 5, we looked at the ways in which a subject's key concepts, key skills and 'range and content' can come together to deepen learning. It is the combination of these three that defines the subject, and ensures the integrity of its discipline.

There is little point in arranging the curriculum in subjects if they are distinguished only by the nature of their information content. They then become mere 'bags of information'. They become true subject disciplines when that knowledge is set in a structure of understanding and skills are developed to pursue new knowledge and apply it. The combination of these three should be at the heart of curriculum design within a subject. Design is not a matter of making a list of all the things students should know and then dividing the list up into lessons. It is a matter of structuring students' understanding.

A deeper understanding

The tension is always between ensuring that young people are inducted properly into a subject's discipline and ensuring that they can also see how one subject fits with another and how consistent elements run through them. Luckily, the two are not at all incompatible. If we see curriculum design as structuring understanding, rather than covering content, then we find that the understanding can often best be arrived at in practical contexts and in combination with other studies. It is in pursuing a subject investigation in concert with another subject that it becomes clear to students what the differences between one subject and another are. Thus, an integrated approach can often clarify subject boundaries rather than blur them.

The process of curriculum design therefore needs to look at those elements that are common across subjects, or which link subjects, or which distinguish one from another. These elements need to be planned in concert across the subjects, and not just left to chance. Then links can be made at each of the three levels of knowledge content, skills and conceptual understanding.

Linking content

In our model of a tree, the branches intertwine so that there are overlaps between art and psychology, or media and sport, and science and history come together in marine archaeology. The key to curriculum design is to identify these points of intertwining and to build them into the curriculum.

At a simple level, students studying erosion in geography might be helped by studying friction and floatation in science. And their understanding of friction and floatation might be enhanced by seeing their impact in the real context of the coast. Are students learning about graphs in maths after they have been using them in history? Are they learning to write reports in English not long after they have been writing reports in science? Are the rivers they are studying in geography the same ones on which battles were fought in history? There is no need to move away from subject teaching in order to make these links clear. It is not difficult to identify them within syllabuses and adjust the timing of those syllabuses to ensure that learning is enhanced. Yet, who is ensuring that these links are being made?

Linking skills

In Chapter 2 we looked at the sort of skills (or, strictly speaking, competencies) that other countries see as running right across the subjects, such as the key skills ('thinking and learning skills') or UNESCO's '4Cs'. These have application in every subject, and so need to be co-ordinated in their introduction, application and development. Again, this does not mean that subjects cannot be taught separately; but it does mean that someone has to take the responsibility for ensuring that these skills are built in at appropriate times and in consistent ways, and that there is an overview of how students are progressing in terms of these skills. Whose responsibility is this in your school?

Linking concepts

There are certain concepts and themes that appear across a wide range of subjects. For example, the notion that developing technology impacts on people's lives might be traced through history, geography, science, citizenship, art, music, literature, ICT and D&T. If such themes or concepts appear in each subject, then it makes sense to ensure that they appear in a coherent way. The implications for design are as above!

An integrated approach

All of this can be done by keeping subjects separate, but by co-ordinating the syllabuses so that the key links are brought out and understood. Many schools have found that once they have established the links and co-ordinated the syllabuses, it becomes easy to integrate the subjects and teach them together. This has the advantage of making the links clear, but may run the danger of students failing to grasp the essence of the different subjects. This can be avoided by building it into the curriculum design. The right learning experiences can ensure that students do understand the key subject distinctions even within an integrated approach.

This integration usually happens at Key Stage 3, and this is where the difference between Key Stages 3 and 4 begins to emerge. The nearer the student gets to the examination world, the less the curriculum tends to be integrated. As they approach Year 10, students start to run in the subject lanes of their exams, the syllabus guiding them to the finishing line. Even where the exam syllabus is a practical one, it is typically separate.

A student's experience therefore becomes a set of courses supported by the requirements on the school such as personal, social, health and citizenship education (PSHCE) or work experience and some optional extras such as sport, a school performance, international exchanges and community activity. The optional extras spice up the whole experience for the student and, perhaps by this stage in their maturity, most are ready to see the importance of meeting the requirements of a series of examinations and feel grown up as they fit together the various aspects of school life.

Many schools, though, believe that students benefit from a curriculum that brings subjects together, and emphasizes the integration of learning. Interestingly, schools that have tried a new development in Year 7 have seen such good outcomes in terms of progress, attitudes, attendance and moral, that they have extended the programme to Year 8. There are plenty of examples now of schools taking the process through into Year 9.

Getting going in school

What are the steps to make something different work? It is clearly essential to ensure that the required subject programmes of study are covered within an integrated approach. But it is also important to remember (as Sinek pointed out in Chapter 1) why we are integrating. It is not just to save time and make things more interesting (although this may also be achieved); it is to bring out the connections between the subjects within a given theme. The connections will be at the level of content, skills and wider concepts. The integration of subjects will also give students the opportunity of looking at the same topic from different angles. It is essential that this is emphasized and made clear. It is the different subject angles, and their associated methodologies, that will clarify to the students the important distinctions between subjects. In Peters (1971) view, there will be different ways of establishing the truth of propositions about the same topic.

So curriculum design needs to focus on the synergies between subjects, but also clarify the different and distinct methodologies they use. This should bring students to a much clearer and deeper understanding of the 'big ideas' and 'key concepts' that structure knowledge. These are Hirsch's (1987) 'schemata' that allow us to make sense of the knowledge that we accrue.

These are the considerations that should lie at the heart of an integrated approach. They are Sinek's 'Why', and are the reason we would want to integrate at all.

Looking for the common elements

Where schools do take an integrated approach, they usually do so through a common theme or title that allows the content of several subjects to be put into a common context. The themes may be things that go beyond the requirements of the subject national curriculum and provide opportunity for skills and attitudes to develop alongside the subject knowledge.

Subject	Elements e.g.	Theme 1 World of work	Theme 2 Resistance	Theme 3 Our community
History	Chronology			
Geography	Location			
Maths	Statistics			
Art	Observation			
Drama	Control			
ICT	Audience			

Figure 6.5 Themes

A matrix, like the one in Figure 6.5, can guide discussion. Each subject lists its essential elements of the programmes of study.

As the grid is completed, it becomes clear which elements of the programmes of study can be met within each integrated theme and whether students will meet, practise or apply their learning. Some essential elements may not fit within the integrated columns. These then, need to be taught separately.

This will leave the school with a combination of integrated and subject-based approaches, and this often has implications for the timetable that we shall look at below.

There is, of course, a complete range of approaches being used, from complete integration of all subjects to exclusively single subject teaching, with most schools being somewhere in between. The Olympic Games school in the example in Chapter 3 was, in a sense, one-fifth integrated. There were traditional subject-based lessons from Monday to Thursday, and then an integration of those subjects on Fridays. Other schools hold a theme week each half term where subjects are integrated around a theme, with traditional subject teaching in between. Other schools arrange the curriculum mainly in themes with a small amount of subject teaching to 'mop up' the bits that do not fit neatly into themes, or to reinforce concepts that were in the themes but were not fully understood.

Timetable implications arise because themed approaches usually require longer periods of study than single subjects. This is not always the case, nor does it need to be the case – and we shall explore this more in Chapter 12. A single subject approach may well have a range of needs with regard to time. Within one subject, some learning might be best accomplished in regular

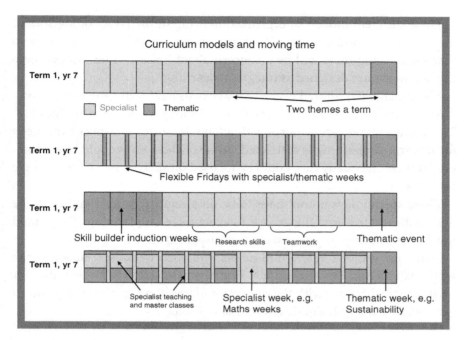

Figure 6.6 Timetable

short bursts over a period of weeks, while other learning might require a sustained effort for a whole day or week. It is not just an integrated approach that needs long time slots. However, for the purposes of this chapter we shall assume that it does.

In Figure 6.6, we can see four possible models for balancing the use of time between themes and specialist teaching to retain the integrity of both and to exploit the mutual benefit of both to the overall learning offer.

Possible organizational structures for teaching the content

In this model, we see that some examples include 'themed' weeks, where skills learned elsewhere are brought together in a focused experience. These are often seen as culminations of work that has been ongoing over time and become significant events for students – and in a sense they are some of the collections of 'leaves and roots' that will stand out in their memories for years to come.

These different models of organization bring in the issues of logistics of teachers, spaces and time use. If certain lessons per week are given over to themed learning there will be a concern about 'missed time', unless these themed weeks are designed as integral to learning.

The timetable is altered every five weeks to have a drop-down day or a 'Wonderful Wednesday', a 'Marvellous Monday' or a 'Terrific Tuesday'. These are separate from normal timetable learning and mean the need for integrated planning is restricted. Some of these days could be on integrated themes; equally they could be focused on specific elements of single subject work.

These special days do not have to be on a regular pattern and could be done with rotated teaching groups to economize on planning. They could involve the whole year group at once or dispersed teaching groups.

Figure 6.7 shows a Year 7 outline plan for such weeks spread across the whole experience. Of course, there is still much to do in the planning for what actually happens with the students and how the logistics of large numbers can be managed. This is referred to in Chapter 12.

Essential Learning Experiences

In order to design compelling learning experiences that will contribute to our school's aims, we commit to 6 thematic weeks a year – these will be problem based, require teamwork and make links across subjects to issues in the real world.

In Year 7 this will include:

Murder mystery	English, art, citizenship, forensic science, media studies
Community makeover	Making a difference- English, citizenship, DT, maths geography, history
Dragon's Den	Young enterprise – DT, English, science, maths
International café	Healthy eating – international cuisine, MFL, DT, music, art, RE
University challenge	Research and presentation on Thurs and Fri, Research a skills Mon to Wed
Alternative Edinburgh Festival	Drama, PE, English, dance, art, enterprise

A formal programme of timetables lessons incorporate the themes and build skills towards a successful implementation of the thematic weeks.

Figure 6.7 Essential learning experiences

As we move on through the year groups, the opportunity to build on the processes and the learning becomes more apparent, especially when schools get good feedback from students and parents. For the school, though, and the curriculum leader in particular, the introduction of new approaches becomes more challenging with natural concerns about proximity to examination syllabus work. Additionally, the staff who now need to be involved will have all sorts of preconceptions based on their understanding of what they think has been happening in Years 7 and 8 for the last two years.

In search of specialism

The branches of the tree subdivide into limbs and then twigs, just as the specialization within a subject discipline grows more marked. So science becomes physics, chemistry and biology, which later become microbiology, astrophysics or genetics. The more a subject is pursued, the more specialized it becomes.

By the end of Key Stage 3, indeed very early within it, many students will have fixed views of their capability, success, failure – and potential. The longer that the door of possibility is left open, the better the chance of success for the student and the lower the possibility of frustration and behaviour challenges for staff. At the point of options, students will reflect on their specialism, often described as preference, aptitude or successes. More likely, they are the areas in which the student has the maximum chance of 'learning survival'.

A specialism should not be what is left when all else has been seen as a failure. Most people set off with high hopes in everything and gradually fall at the hurdles that they meet, leaving just a few subjects still standing as option time approaches. This is the 'Grand National' view of the curriculum. Everyone starts off together and follows the same course, but the fences become more and more difficult and many fall or become 'refusers'. By the end, very few are still going, so they are the true subject specialists, and so can go to university.

A true specialism builds with immersion, with being captivated and self-challenged. It comes from pride and confidence in the subject arena; with a quest for more scope and depth. Specialism comes from exploring new contexts and setting our own course of study and being recognized and referred to by peers as a developing expert.

Do we practise so that we can apply skills or practise to prove we are competent? Do we work to see what mark the teacher gives us so that we can measure ourselves against our new peer group, to find our place in the learning pecking order?

These questions influence the outlook and attitudes of a new group of learners with varying aspirations, varying confidence and varying outlooks on learning. They will engage with stories of famous people and events, they will associate with places near and far and people like and different from them; they will be fascinated by the changing world around them, the patterns and the problems. They will want to express the knowledge they are gathering in many forms: in maps, pictures, photographs, websites, models, plays and dance. They will want to make things, grow things and say things. They will write if it matters and someone is genuinely going to read the efforts.

The search for specialism occurs at a much earlier age in England than elsewhere. This is historical and cultural, but also to do with our image of teaching and learning and what schools are trying to do. Are we fishing with lines, trying to find the few historians, few mathematicians or scientists? Or do we try to get as many as possible to build their specialism by fishing with nets? Is the learning journey a route march with people dropping exhausted and demoralized along the way? Or is it an orienteering challenge, with markers to be visited in any order and downhill slopes within the uphill struggles through the undergrowth of problems?

Within subject departments we often see Key Stage 3 as a preparation for the GCSE and 'A' Level courses to come, yet outside of the compulsory subjects, the great majority of students do not go on to take these courses at all. In most schools, 80 per cent of students taking geography, history, D&T, art or music do not pursue their studies beyond the end of Year 9 (QCA Annual Reports 2006–09). So are we preparing them to be specialists, or is Key Stage 3 the time when we should be rounding off their studies of these subjects so that we can send them out into the world with all they need to cope? This is a great responsibility when you consider that as adults most people's leisure time is taken up visiting other countries, going to museums, engaged in crafts or repair work on their houses, or listening to music. Is this being a specialist?

Under the canopy

This brings us back to the canopy of leaves. Is it the individual leaves that are important, or the total effect of the canopy? Are we keeping in mind the need to prepare young people for life ahead, as well as to prepare them for a GCSE examination? Have we remembered the roots of the curriculum tree and the importance of the competencies that not only deepen understanding within the subjects, but that will sustain lifelong learning?

It is these competencies that we shall be looking at in the next chapter.

Building in the competencies

Levels of Satisfaction

A selective school had a long history of high attainment in terms of passes at GCSE with 100 per cent of students gaining five A*–C passes. Most students gained far more than five passes, and most of these were at A and A*. Would you be satisfied with that?

Interestingly, this school was still dissatisfied. Although the students worked hard and did very well indeed in terms of GCSE passes, the school was concerned that they lacked the ability to work independently. They were not self managers, team workers, creative thinkers, independent enquirers or reflective learners (have you heard those terms before?). So they may have a good suite of qualifications at 16, but not the skills and competencies to prepare them for work or further study.

So the school was keen to change its curriculum to build in the development of these skills, but was equally keen to maintain its 100 per cent GCSE record. But were the two compatible?

The staff were in agreement on the need for change, and heads of departments agreed on its importance. Then came the crunch. 'So who is going to teach these skills?' 'I don't have the time to teach all those, I have the syllabus to get through!' and, 'Why can't they do them in PSHCE or Tutor-time?'

So, everyone agreed that the students need to learn these things, but no one saw it as their responsibility to teach them.

In Chapter 2, we suggested that a competency was a combination of:

The competencies could be subject specific or generic. In the latter case the knowledge and understanding would come from a range of subjects, and the skill would be applicable in each of them. There are two significant issues here for curriculum design. First, they won't just happen of their own accord, so schools need to be active in promoting them. Second, students will build these up across the whole curriculum so there needs to be a system of co-ordination.

While designing the curriculum *within* a subject might be fairly straightforward, ensuring a coherent programme of generic skills and competencies *across* a range of subjects is a much harder challenge. Of course, much of this challenge comes from the way in which secondary schools are traditionally organized. In English primary schools, where one teacher is usually responsible for all the subjects for a class, it is much easier to design experiences that involve more than one subject, easier to build up key skills and competencies across different subjects, and much easier to vary the timetable from day to day and week to week to give emphasis to one subject or another.

This does not mean that it is impossible to do this in secondary schools, or even that it is necessary to vary the timetable. There are three issues:

1. Building the generic skills and competencies into the subject programmes.
2. Ensuring that the programme of competency development is coherent, so that the work in one subject complements the work in another.
3. Providing a coherent overall programme that ensures progress as students move through the school.

The issue of coherence in competencies is not really different from the need for coherence across subjects even without taking account of competencies. Where each subject pursues programmes in isolation there is always the danger of fragmentation, with students failing to see the connections between learning in one subject and another. This is not just a matter of seeing connections, but also failing to take advantage of the way in which learning in one subject can reinforce and extend learning in another.

	Eng	Ma	Sci	Hist	Geog	Art	Mus	ICT	DT	MFL	PE	Cit
Problem solving		X	X			X	X		X			
Team work												
Critical thinking												
Creativity												
Commun-ication												

Figure 7.1 The matrix

This is particularly important in the area of skills and competencies where the development is taking place within a particular knowledge base.

The school in the opening scenario worked through departments. It became apparent to everyone from the initial response that there had to be a co-ordinated approach. Surely problem solving happens in maths anyway? And D&T. Does no one else solve problems? What about art or music or science? Taking this approach they worked through the subjects and constructed a grid very similar to the one in Chapter 4 (see Figure 7.1).

They started filling in the grid to allocate a competency to each subject, but soon found that, of course, all the competencies are features of all the subjects. So the grid could actually be filled in with a cross in every box.

This left them with a further issue – if you say that the competencies are developed everywhere, then the danger is that no one takes responsibility, and they may end up being developed nowhere. The school saw two models:

1. Allocating each competency to a number of departments, so, for example, if there are 4 competencies and 12 subject departments, each competency is developed in 3 departments.

2. Each department develops all of the competencies, but with a recognition that some lend themselves more to one competency than to another.

The disadvantage of the first model is that the competencies (whichever ones you choose) are not isolated from one another. It is hard to be in a team without communicating, and hard to solve a problem without thinking critically. Attempts to define competencies as being completely separate from one another have generally been unsuccessful. It is much more useful to see them as a range of skills and attitudes that can be deployed in a variety of knowledge contexts. The competencies can be seen as attempts to define elements of this range, but there will always be overlaps.

Therefore it is almost impossible for a department to develop one competency while a different department develops another competency.

This is particularly the case if we are following the model set out in Chapter 3 where the 'roots' are blended with the 'leaves' in the 'trunk' of students' learning experiences. The focus on competencies will vary with the particular piece of learning within the subject. For example, the work on the beach leant itself to a focus on investigation and problem solving. Another aspect of geography might have been more appropriate for communication or creativity. The making of the animated film leant itself to teamwork and creativity, but another aspect of ICT would be more appropriate for some other competency.

Allocating separate competencies to different departments will not work if the competencies are being fully integrated into learning, because it will not be possible to separate them in practice. And if they are not being integrated, they will not be successful. If a competency is a combination of knowledge, understanding, skills and attitude, then an integrated approach is essential.

This also raises questions about the approach of the whole school focusing on one competency per term. The same issue about integration arises. If the science unit is about investigation, then it would be odd either to focus on communication, or to change the order of the units just to fit with the competency focus.

However, the integrated approach does raise the need for co-ordination. If departments are focusing on those competencies that fit with their programmes, then there is a danger that, overall, some are being missed or that the emphasis becomes distorted. There is always some flexibility in curriculum design that would allow a change of emphasis within a unit, but a department would not know that one was needed unless someone within the school is taking the overview. For example, we suggested in Chapter 4 that the geography unit on the beach could have taken different directions, developing investigation or communication with a slight adjustment of the focus on the knowledge domain. This is almost always the case, but who is going to provide the information to departments that enables them to make these adjustments? Who would it be in your school?

It might fall to the Curriculum Deputy, or might be part of the Head of Year role. Whoever it is, someone needs to exercise the overview of competency development and be able to help shape the direction of design within departments. This might be a radical step for some schools, and some departments might not be easy with such a departure, but it is a necessary step to make this work.

Departments that have not been expected to develop generic competencies before tend to see them initially as a distraction from the proper work of teaching the syllabus. However, as we pointed out in Chapter 4, the linking of the knowledge base of the syllabus to the competencies has the effect of extending and deepening that knowledge. It also has the effect of making learning more active and engaging. Once departments start working in this way, they do eventually see the benefits (even if 'eventually' seems a long time in some cases!).

Progress in competencies

Agreeing on a list of competencies, or even working out how to integrate them into learning is not the end of the matter. A title such as 'problem solving' is not sufficient in itself. Other questions arise: What do we mean by problem solving? Are there different aspects to it? How does that work in different subjects? Is problem solving in maths the same as problem solving in art or science? Does problem solving develop as students get older? What should we expect from a student in Year 7 or Year 11?

The complex relationship between skills and knowledge

Competencies clearly need to develop, and they need to develop in the context of the knowledge bases within which they are located. Hirsch (1987) has cast doubt in the ability of a skill to exist outside of a knowledge context. Although Hirsch's work was published some time ago, he is much quoted at the moment in the skills versus knowledge debate, so is worth considering in the context. His original work in literacy suggested that students' ability to perform skills such as summing up the main points or structuring a piece of writing varied with the amount of knowledge they had of the subject matter. For example, a student who knew all about fishing was much better at picking the main points from an article in an angling magazine, than from a piece about ballet. Unfortunately, some people (including Hirsch himself) have taken his original thesis to mean that skills don't matter at all and only knowledge counts. His original work points to the more complex relationship between skills and knowledge contexts and the way in which skills develop through them:

> Research demonstrates that the ability of humans to exercise a skill depends on their possession of specific 'schemata' that are sufficiently numerous and detailed to handle the many varieties of task they are called upon to perform. (1987)

The 'schemata' are sets of understanding about how the world operates that are built up through increasing knowledge and the 'key concepts' referred to in Chapter 5. These central understandings enable knowledge to be acquired, processed and understood. We have pointed out that it is often deficiencies in these schemata that make it difficult for some students to understand new material, however cogently and clearly it is presented. Hirsch here is suggesting that it is not just the extent of the knowledge, but the way in which it is organized within the mind that enables it to be manipulated. This manipulation is, of course, a skill.

To support his argument, Hirsch quotes an early experiment by De Groot (1965) in which he showed people a ten second glimpse of a chess board with 25 pieces on it, and then asked them to recall the position of all the pieces. When the pieces were arranged in the positions of an actual game, expert chess players had 100 per cent success while non chess players struggled to place five pieces. However, when the pieces were arranged randomly on the board, both experts and non players fared equally badly. Hirsch concludes that the skill of memory is dependent on familiarity with the structure of the knowledge being recalled. The expert chess players had a way of understanding the positions on the board and how one piece related to another in the context of a game. They had a schema by which to organize the information and so could recall it. People without such a schema could not organize the information and so could not recall it.

It is not so clear that this applies to all skills in the same way. Some skills have a common set of processes that have more common applications. For example, there might be a methodology of scientific investigation that might be applied in a wide variety of contexts. This might be different from the methodology needed to investigate historical contexts, but both would have wide applications. The same might be true of a competency such as teamwork. The way a team works together in sport might be different from the cast of a play or the team running the Hadron Collider, or running the kitchen in a restaurant. However, within each context there is a common set of processes that enable people to work effectively as a team.

Back to Hirsch's memory example, there are plenty of methods for improving your memory that work by using some sort of generic schema that can be applied in a wide variety of situations. People imagine they are walking through a house and ascribe bits of information to different rooms, then retrace their steps to recall the information. This general application of a skill seems to run contrary to Hirsch.

Even within Hirsch's analysis, it is necessary to develop knowledge in an ordered and meaningful way so that schemata are developed. We have seen that learning in the context of skills extends and develops knowledge in a way that makes sense to the learner. If information is gained in a rote way without a grasp of the overall significance and meaning, then the schemata will not be developed. This is the central argument for learning that is joined-up, meaningful and within the context of the learner's experience. It needs to start with the learner's existing schemata and then challenge and extend them. This is true learning and not just the acquisition of information. The acquisition of new information is central to the process, but is not sufficient in itself.

What does all this mean for progress in competencies?

The complex relationship between skill and knowledge context means that the greater the variety of contexts in which the skills are developed, the greater the development of the skills. The two cannot be divorced. The variety needs to involve depth and complexity as well as range.

In Chapter 12 we shall look in more detail at the way in which progress in competencies can be assessed, and it implications for design. Most schools look at how the competencies apply in the different subjects and how they fit with the existing subject expectation. Both the national curriculum and the exam board syllabi have expectations that go beyond the acquisition of knowledge, so this is usually a fruitful way of looking at levels of demand or performance.

There are numerous 'skills ladders' in circulation that take skills and tease them out into a series of levels or progressive steps. The problem with these is that they tend to divorce the skills from the knowledge context, and although one might not agree entirely with Hirsch, the knowledge contexts are important in defining skill development. And it is the joining of the knowledge context to the skill, along with the necessary attitude, that develops the competency.

Making it work in school

The school in the opening scenario took an approach that sought to develop competencies within the existing subject structure but which built in a system of progress co-ordination across those subjects. Other schools have applied different models with equal success.

Some schools have concerns about competencies being entirely subject-centred and are worried that competencies developed this way may not be easily applied out of those contexts. They have therefore been keen to set up different cross-subject contexts in which the competencies can be developed and deployed.

One approach is the one used in the Olympic Games example in Chapter 3. The school pursued its usual subject-centred timetable from Monday to Thursday, but created rich situations for the development of competencies on Fridays. This did not mean that competencies were ignored for the rest of the week. Competencies involve knowledge as well as skills and young people must learn both. And this is what lessons are for!

There is a wide variation of the Friday theme. Some call them 'Freaky Fridays' or say they are 'off timetable' or even 'off curriculum'. Yet these sort of experiences are very much part of the curriculum, and they have been timetabled for Friday. And it does not have to be Friday, of course!

Many schools have found that attendance on such Fridays is higher than any other day of the week. And surely there is a message here. There is something about these experiences and this way of learning that resonates with young people.

A variation on this approach is to designate a week at the end of each half term to these sorts of open-ended group activities where students have an opportunity to develop and deploy a wide range of competencies. These weeks might have single subject focus, but generally give more scope for active and co-operative learning than formal lessons.

A more radical approach, taken up by an increasing number of schools is to extend the Freaky Friday to a whole year. If you have not come across this before, it may seem unlikely, but many schools are following a 'competency-based' programme in Year 7, and then completing the Key Stage 3 programme of study in two years. The argument runs that that these competencies are very important to learning, and when students are good at investigating, critical thinking, co-operating and communicating, they find learning easier. So why don't we really focus on these competencies for a year and then the students will fly through the Key Stage 3 programmes? Some schools are using programmes such as RSA's 'Opening Minds' as a basis for the work, much of which is thematic and exploratory and has similar elements to a primary school approach. Some schools see this as an added benefit to transition. Some have even recruited teachers experienced in primary schools to help with this programme.

Of course, these Opening Minds-type years cannot be devoid of a knowledge base, and it would be perverse, anyway, to ignore the opportunities to explore aspects of the Key Stage 3 programmes. The 3Cs are much in evidence and these are often seen as the key focus for the year because it is often the lack of these competencies that prevent students from learning across the curriculum. So, whatever the title of the years, weeks or days, Skills Week, or Competency-based Year, there is never an absence of knowledge development. The approach works best when thought is given to the design of that knowledge so that there is clear development of competencies through the contexts.

The fact that all these schools report ongoing success indicates that there is not just one way of doing things. A common factor in the success is that the approach is not just confined to the Fridays or theme week or Year 7. There is the danger in these approaches that everyone thinks that they don't have to bother with competencies because they will be covered on Fridays or in theme weeks. In the most successful schools, the approach continues in the subject lessons. The development of the skills is in the immediate context of the knowledge with the reciprocal benefits. The Fridays or theme weeks become wider and extended contexts for competencies, not the students' only chance of developing them.

One hundred percent 5A*–Cs

The successful students in the select school of the opening scenario carried on with their 100 per cent pass rate, but added the extra bonus of the competencies that they had developed. One of the unintended consequences was that they started to do much better at 'A' Level. The competencies of investigation and critical thinking, working independently and solving problems, stood them in good stead for the different kind of work. The approach has not been going on long enough to track students through university, but initial signs are good. We often worry about transition from one phase to another, but the development of competencies across the school can be very effective. The schools pursuing a 'skills-based' Year 7 report the same benefit for transition.

The more predictable consequence was that the sorts of learning experiences that build in competences were actually much more interesting and engaging. In fact, these provided the sort of learning the students could not resist. And 'irresistible learning' is the subject of the next chapter.

8 Making learning irresistible

Clued Up

Clad in cotton overalls and surgical gloves, the team is painstakingly picking its way through the house. Each item is photographed and examined in detail. No detail is missed, no stone is left unturned. But all the details need to add up to a coherent overall picture. Has a crime been committed here? What has happened? Can we work out who was responsible? Forensic knowledge must be deployed, and forensic skills must be applied to gather evidence which must then be analysed, synthesized and evaluated.

No prizes for guessing that the team is made up of students. They are Year 10s following a BTEC course in forensic science. The house is the one used by the local police force in its training programme, and this is a joint project between the police and a school whose students are not always well disposed towards the police or to learning.

There is something about the situation, however, that these reluctant learners find hard to resist.

What example would you use to illustrate irresistible learning? Would it be a lesson, event, routine or something that happened out of hours? Would it be something wonderfully exciting, whizz-bang and totally out of the ordinary? Or would it something simple and well crafted, or a combination of things?

The phrase 'making learning irresistible' is frequently used by schools to denote an aspiration to design learning experiences so constructed that students cannot help but learn, but most people think in terms of the excitement rather than the construction.

Many of the examples of learning experiences given so far in this book are of experiences that have some excitement, that are always engaging, but that also structure learning. The students on the beach were enjoying the outing, but the nature of the investigation was so constructed that they were inevitably involved in the higher-order expectations of geography and science. Engagement is essential, excitement would be very helpful, but neither would be sufficient in itself if there was no element of curriculum design structuring the experience in such a way that learning became inevitable.

The students writing the Olympic bids in Chapter 3 enjoyed the teamwork and the competitive element of the enterprise (they also enjoyed buying their teachers' advice), but in order to complete the bids they had to make use of and combine a complex range of learning from different subjects and develop a high level of skills from the 'roots'. The other important part of the structure was that there was an immediate opportunity to use the skill in a practical situation for a 'real' purpose. Part of the irresistibility was that the students did not only gain a theoretical understanding in lessons, they also gained practical understanding in the team situations.

The fact that we are trying to create 'irresistible learning' implies that there must be some other kind of learning currently – presumably 'resistible learning'. This must be learning that students can 'resist' in some way. So, what makes learning irresistible? Either the students choose not to resist, or could not resist even if they wanted to. This learning would be like eating an extra chocolate – 'I just couldn't resist!' So one way of seeking to identify the features of irresistibility would be to list the reasons why students might instead choose to resist. This has been carried out with countless students – asking the question both ways – and the list of reasons not to learn is always fairly similar:

- It's boring
- I can't see the point
- I can't understand it

- It's too hard
- I'm fed up with writing
- No one ever helps you

Asking students what makes a good teacher, results in a similar list (in reverse). Students often have a very good idea of what works for them. A good teacher:

- Makes it interesting for you
- Explains things clearly
- Listens to you and treats you with respect (doesn't get cross and shout)
- Helps you when you're stuck
- Gives you time to finish

The key to the students' analysis is that learning needs to be interesting, not just by being about something interesting, but also in the way that learning unfolds and gives the students something interesting to do (usually other than to just listen or write). Students like to see the point of the learning; it has to have some relevance to them and their lives (Goswami & Bryant 2007). There seems to be a trade-off between interest and need. If they see a real need to learn something then they seem willing to put up with it being less interesting; if it is really exciting, then they don't need to see the point at all, because being excited is point enough. The interest needs to be linked to clear explanations. It is important that the learning takes place in a supportive environment; stress over not understanding things, getting things wrong and not having enough time is not conducive to learning.

A wider whole

Many aspects come together to make learning irresistible. Exciting experiences by themselves do not constitute irresistible learning, neither do cogent explanations that fail to interest the student. A visit to McDonalds will excite many students but will not, of itself, constitute irresistible learning. The most lucid explanation will not work with students who have fallen asleep through boredom.

So, there may be a number of factors in making learning irresistible, not just one magic key to unlock learning. These constitute the 'quality' aspect of curriculum design, as opposed to the 'functional' aspect. We may design experiences that will achieve our aims, but the question is how well they do so. We don't want to design learning experiences that are adequate, we want to design experiences that are compelling and make learning irresistible.

Of course, the nature of the irresistibility must depend upon the nature of the learning intended. Learning a skill such as handwriting might need a very different set of experiences from the development of caring attitudes towards wildlife, or the understanding of abstract concepts of equivalence in algebra. But although the cases are different, they have features in common.

Getting back to traditional methods

In his own engaging conference presentations, Trevor Hawes has suggested that if we want to make learning really engaging for students, then we must 'get back to traditional methods'. But he turns the clock a long way back to get to those methods. He points out that for most of human history we have learned from other members of the family or tribe. We learned things that were essential to our way of life: hunting, lighting fires, building shelters, cooking, storing food, etc. We learned in practical ways by engaging in the actual tasks. We learned holistically without the learning being broken down into discrete steps. Above all, we had a strong emotional commitment to learning. Our brains have evolved to learn in this way over thousands of years.

Learning in classrooms from strangers not part of our tribe (for the most part), while sitting with 30 other students of exactly our age and listening to the stranger talk, is far from a traditional method of learning. It is, as Hawes points out, a 'new-fangled experiment in learning that is not working out very well so far'.

The features that Hawes picks out as being part of the 'traditional methods' to which our brains are attuned are:

- Learning as a group experience
- Relevance to the learner's life
- Active involvement

- Learning in a practical situation
- An holistic approach
- Emotional commitment to learning

This is very similar to the set of features identified by the students themselves – perhaps it really is the way their brains have developed! But how do we build these features into our design?

Exciting students' imaginations

We would not be very ambitious about our curriculum if we sought merely to interest the students, or even to excite them. Exciting their imaginations takes learning a step further. This does not have to be an exercise in fantasy, but could involve imagining different solutions to problems or ways of expressing things. The students writing the Olympic bids had their imaginations excited by the possibilities inherent in the bids. The students commissioning the statue had to explore a range of options for attaining their goal and came up with some imaginative solutions. The more open-ended the experience we design, the more possibilities there are and the more scope there is for creative responses.

Irresistible learning is not a drudge. It finds ways of uplifting the spirit as well as the mind. It finds ways of making necessary practice enthralling. It excites students with the prospect of writing a bid, or with solving a crime. It brings the GCSE maths to life.

Fitting with how students learn

In Chapter 6, we looked at the different ways in which students acquire knowledge, skills and understanding, so one key way of making the curriculum fit the way students learn is to take account of the type of learning involved. But we can go beyond this. There has been considerable progress in research into how the human brain functions, and there is a growing literature about the implications this research has for education and the curriculum (for example, Katzir & Pare-Blagoev 2006, Fischer & Immordino-Yang 2008, Goswami 2008, Wolfe 2010). Neurologists do not claim to know entirely how the learning process works, but some points have emerged, many of which seem to line up with professional wisdom:

- Learning involves the making of new connections in the neural pathways. These are physical changes made within the brain in response to external stimuli (seeing, hearing, feeling things, etc.).
- This process is holistic rather than linear (there is no one particular neural line that enables you to do long division).
- The wider the range of stimuli the greater the learning (listening is not always the best way of learning, especially for young people).
- The brain is capable of making hundreds of new connections every second (even though you may think you have some students who haven't made a new connection in weeks).
- Skills learned in context are more likely to be able to be performed in that context.
- Emotional engagement (being interested, being excited, seeing the point) seems to help connections being formed.
- Stress gets in the way of learning.

Such considerations form the basis of most of the examples we have looked at through this book. Holistic learning with a range of stimuli, learning in context and strong emotional engagement have been features of experiences from the Olympic Games example to the one with the students on the beach.

We know from much earlier writings on learning such as Vygotsky (1978) that students are active learners, not only in the physical sense, but in seeking to make meaning of new experiences. This is corroborated by more recent work such as Gardner (1999) and Goswami and Bryant (2007). Students need to be active rather than passive in their involvement in learning. They need to have something to do, something to explore or investigate or create. Listening is a way of absorbing some information, but it seldom leads to deeper understanding without more active engagement.

Fitting with adolescence

A hundred years ago, young people left school at 12 years old and were seen as adults by 14. By 16 they were men and women, not 'young people'. Now, young people grow up quicker, but stay young longer. Twelve year olds have a superficial level of sophistication that their great-grandparents would not have recognized. Yet at 16, instead of being an adult at work, they are still children at school. The tensions this produces are with us everyday.

Learning can become all too resistible when it bears no relation to students' own stage of emotional as well as intellectual development, when it makes no connection to their concerns and interests, their hopes and aspirations, or when it fails to address their dreads and fears. Without these connections, learning is unlikely to engage their interest, excite their imaginations or awaken their natural curiosity and desire to learn. The sort of learning that is easiest to resist is a curriculum that is a long list of disconnected things to learn, and which students cannot see the point of. This does not mean that students don't have to learn them, or that they need to be 'dumbed-down' to make them learnable. In fact, it could be argued that disconnecting learning from its context and teaching it as things to be learned for an exam is the real 'dumbing-down'. The students writing the Olympic bid or investigating erosion were facing challenges to extend their knowledge and understanding and to take their learning deeper through application, analysis and synthesis. This is rigorous learning.

In the trade-off we referred to earlier, students are often willing to trade interest and relevance because they see the necessity of a qualification, but this can also limit the depth of learning. A Year 10 student in a GCSE French class was studying the pluperfect tense. When asked when she would use this tense (a question aimed at eliciting her understanding of its role) she said, 'In the GCSE exam'. When it becomes difficult to engage students' natural curiosity it is helpful to have the alternative motivator of the qualifications. The student is learning the pluperfect tense, not because she ever wants to use it or can see the point of it in communicating with French people, but because she needs a good grade at GCSE. This works at the institutional level of keeping the students on task and committed to a form of success. But the trade-off for the institutional level is that students' compliance is often obtained at the price of a commitment to learning for its intrinsic value. Of course, no one would want to jeopardize the gaining of essential qualifications; the point is that a curriculum that resonates with the context of students' own needs can enhance learning and so lead to better performance in examinations. When learning becomes irresistible, students learn more, and when they learn more they do better in tests!

Many of the examples we have looked at involve open-ended situations where students are given scope to explore different avenues of learning. This learning is seldom linear, and so it is more difficult to be sure exactly what it will be and to keep track of it. However, it does resonate more with how the human brain and the teenage mind work. Learning in this model is almost incidental to the experience rather than a meticulously planned series of information to be recalled at a later stage. This makes metacognitive awareness of one's own learning more difficult, but although there are certainly times when it is helpful to be aware of what we are learning and to think about how we are going about it, there are also times when the sheer joy of finding things out should be allowed to take over. The more complex the situation, and the richer the learning, the less possible it is to be metacognitively aware of all that is going on. If the brain is making hundreds of new connections every minute, we cannot keep track of them all. We can be aware of some simple lines of superficial learning and keep track of that, but the complexity of deep learning will always elude our conscious minds.

Resonating with the students' own lives

For many students, what goes on in school bears little relation to their own lives or what goes on outside of school. Most seem to accept this parallel universe where values and concerns are so different, and where even what counts as knowledge can also be different. They accept it, but the disjuncture impacts on their learning. If the curriculum does not connect with students' lives, it will leave them behind. On the other hand, the curriculum cannot merely wrap itself around the students' lives. It must widen their horizons and increase their realization of all the possibilities that are open to them. But the curriculum cannot do this if it has left them behind at the very start.

Authentic learning

The approach to learning is an integral part of curriculum design as it shapes the learning experience, and helps engage and motivate students. Students learn best when they:

- engage in *authentic* tasks with a clear purpose and *audience*,
- see that it is *worth learning*,

- derive *satisfaction* from the experience,
- are able to make a *contribution* and see that their bit matters,
- *produce* something of which they can be proud,
- have *time* to explore a topic and complete their work,
- receive *clear explanations* and *supportive feedback*.

The power of presenting to an actual audience is huge. We do not always have to go outside of the school to find them. If there are 200 students in a year group in 8 groups of 25, the potential for authentic audiences is as big as the permutations. The potential for subgroups to be producing work to show to other subgroups or to the half year or whole year group is massive and can do wonders for motivation. This is especially if the other groups have covered different content within an extended theme.

How to use audiences therefore becomes part of the planning of time use, and the move away from teacher transmission starts to be more secure. To whom might students in Year 9 show their work? The film-makers in the Chapter 6 scenario had a very wide audience – their DVD sold around the town. It was their awareness of this wide and real audience that drove their desire to make their work the best it could possibly be. It drove them to combine the history with the English of the voiceover, the music in the background, the graphic design of the photographs and the ICT of the film itself. Members of the public expect such a combination for ideas to be communicated effectively.

The biggest breakthrough in learning approaches, and leaf acquisition, comes when we consider *what* the students might communicate to the range of audiences. This is more than a particular teaching approach; it is a way of integrating understanding in order to present it to an audience. It is, in Bloom's terms, the *application* of learning that is likely to need analysis and synthesis and even the creative putting together of learning in order to present it to someone else. This is the true deepening of learning.

There is sometimes a fear that an integrated approach will detract from subject learning, but approached systematically, it will enhance subject learning. In Chapter 3, we looked at the Olympic Games example where subjects were taught separately from Monday to Thursday, and were then put together in a very structured way on Friday. The students commissioning the statue in Chapter 1, and those running the restaurant in Chapter 2, were also combining a range of subjects, but in a less structured way. All of the scenarios involved students in an authentic (or 'realistic') task that provided the structure for their learning. This structural aspect of the curriculum is often ignored in the process of curriculum design. The way in which students engage with their learning – the actual activities in which they engage – will impact on and structure their learning, and so is an essential part of curriculum design. These activities will organize the way in which subjects are understood, and the way in which the connections between subjects are perceived.

Practical and first-hand

All of the examples we have looked at have been of students engaged in first-hand practical experiences. This does not mean that all learning experiences need to be like this; indeed, there were times within the examples when the students were looking things up on the internet or in books, or listening to experts on a course, or listening to explanations from their teacher. For learning to be irresistible, it does not have to be the same all the time. Modulation, variety and fitness for purpose are part of irresistibility. There will be times when students are sitting and listening to their teachers. There will also be opportunities for:

- open-ended situations where students co-operate with each other to solve problems,
- focused whole-class or group subject teaching,
- independent study,
- coaching and mentoring,
- time for reflection and consolidation.

The key is to ensure that the experience is appropriate to the intended learning.

Over the course of a learning experience, all the forms may come into play. Irresistibility is in the long term and not just in the moment.

The scene of the crime

There was some concern before running the BTEC in forensic science that it would be giving potential villains all the information they needed to ensure that their future crimes would go undetected! In the event it had the much more positive effect of improving relationships between the students and the local police. In fact, several of the students decided that, far from the life of crime that they might otherwise have contemplated, they wanted to join the police force. This then gave them added motivation to work for the GCSEs about which they had previously been at best half-hearted.

The Crime House setting certainly captured the students' interest and made them keen to learn. They wrote reports without complaint, were meticulous in the notes they made, and diligent in their investigations. They listened attentively to the detectives setting up the scenarios and wanted to do well. But in addition to motivation and engagement, there was the careful building up of forensic knowledge and skills, and also the spin-off into other subjects: English, maths and science. The desire to succeed in the forensics area made it impossible to resist the associated learning in other subjects.

Irresistible design

One of the features we have looked at in irresistible learning is the linking of learning to the local context. The curriculum that does not connect with students' own lives and experiences will be all too easy to resist. National expectations must be located firmly in local settings. This means the personal reality of the students, but also the geographical locality of the school.

We explore this further in the next chapter.

9 Local contexts

> **The Humber Bridge**
> If you want to know how long the Humber Bridge is, or how many tons of steel and concrete went into its construction, what forces are acting on the towers, or what stresses on the cables, just ask Year 8 in the nearby school.
>
> The bridge was the focus of work in several subjects. They worked out the inherent forces and stresses in science, considered alternative designs in D&T, investigated the impact on transport and the economy in geography, calculated amounts and shapes in maths, found out how the decision was taken to build it and how it was financed in citizenship.
>
> When they walked over the bridge with the school, it was the first time most of the students had been on it, even though they lived so close.

National expectations in a local context

Schools often feel that they are constrained by the national curriculum and so can't make use of the local environment. Or they feel that they have so much to get through that there is no time to go out and look at what's on the doorstep. Neither needs be the case.

If we look at what the present English National Curriculum actually says (have you done that recently?) you will find that it gives much more scope than people generally think. Here are some examples:

- *D&T*: 'study the behaviour of structural elements in a variety of materials'
- *Science*: 'forces are interactions between objects that can affect their shape and motion'
- *Geography*: 'explore real and relevant contemporary contexts'
- *Maths*: 'work on problems that arise in other subjects and in contexts beyond the school'
- *Citizenship*: 'take into account legal, moral, economic, environmental, historical and social dimensions of political problems and issues'

All of the requirements listed above can be met better outside a classroom than inside. And, of course, they were all met in the context of the Humber Bridge.

There are two points here. First, the Programmes of study are not so lengthy or so detailed that they do not allow time to go out of the classroom. In fact you can read right through the Key Stage 3 programmes of study and wonder how you are going to fill 3 years, let alone whether you will have time to go out. Second, most of the elements within the Programmes of Study could be better learned outside the classroom anyway. And if you combine the two, it is hard to see why you might ever be in the classroom at all.

The Programmes of Study are not straightjackets that can only be learned in one way. They are almost all open-ended requirements that can be met in a variety of ways. You could 'study structural elements' in the context of the Humber Bridge if you were in Humberside, but if you were in London you might be looking at the Olympic Stadia. Wherever you are there will be a context lending itself to the requirements. The same is true of the requirements in every subject. Curriculum design is a matter of looking for the optimum contexts for learning. These are almost always practical, real, first-hand and right on your doorstep. All you need to do is take a requirement and think where in your local environment the learning might take place.

Local needs and opportunities

The local opportunities are not just bridges or buildings; they are all the places, people, resources and events that can be harnessed to bring learning to life. As well as the opportunities arising in our local environment, there are often needs that are particular to a locality. These might be to do with raising aspiration in a deprived area, improving interethnic understanding in a mixed community or widening horizons where experiences are narrow.

A school in Bristol was concerned that its students lacked any pride in their own city, and so it worked with its local primary schools to promote civic pride as a key element of its curriculum. As it turned out, this need opened up a whole world of opportunities. The school's thinking started from the (quite correct!) assumption that it could only be ignorance that would prevent anyone being proud of Bristol. Therefore the curriculum must allow the students to find out much more about the city. There are two ways of doing this: we could run a special unit of study on Bristol and its heritage, or we could look for ways of including it in a whole range of other learning experiences. This does not necessarily mean 'shoehorning' it into inappropriate places, but of taking account of the rich local opportunities that might otherwise be missed.

Local opportunities

In the Bristol example, the schools started by making a list of opportunities presented by the city, which became a list of experiences not to be missed. This was a list of things that no young person should reach the age of 16 without having experienced. The list included famous Bristol features such as: the Suspension Bridge, SS Great Britain, Exploratory Museum, Clifton Downs and Christmas Steps. It also included lesser known features such as the floating harbour, Cabot's ship *The Matthew*, the observatory and the pub of which Long John Silver was the landlord. There were also Bristol themes about which everyone should know, such as chocolate, the history of slavery, aircraft and the making of Wallace and Gromit.

The list becomes an 'arena of opportunities'. The next part of the process was to match the forecast of possibilities to an aspect of the programmes of study. For example, the suspension bridge lends itself to D&T and history. The floating harbour is ideal for science as well as D&T (flotation as well as hydraulics) and also for history. There were also possibilities for citizenship because both bridge and harbour required local decisions to be made and finance to be raised.

Having done this, the school then allocated the opportunities to each year group to ensure that none was missed. This did not prevent other year groups benefiting from the opportunity (in fact, revisiting sites and themes was specifically built into the design). The process was rather like the one in Chapter 3, but with a different centre (see Figure 9.1).

This was the Bristol map of local opportunities not to be missed. What would your local map look like? The Bristol experiences then provided contexts for four elements of learning in the same way as the Chapter 3 model (see Figure 9.1).

If you have never heard of Bristol's floating harbour it can only be a fault in the curriculum of the school where you were a student! It was one of the amazing achievements of Victorian engineering to construct a permanent mooring for great ships miles up a narrow and very tidal river. It is not as visible as the Clifton Suspension Bridge, but in many ways more impressive.

The element missing from Figure 9.2 is the development of civic pride. This was really a natural outcome of any study of the floating harbour, whether the study was historical, scientific or technological (see Figure 9.3).

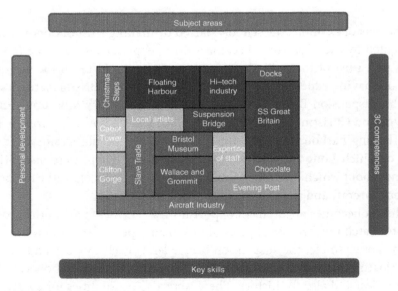

Figure 9.1 The Bristol 'arena'

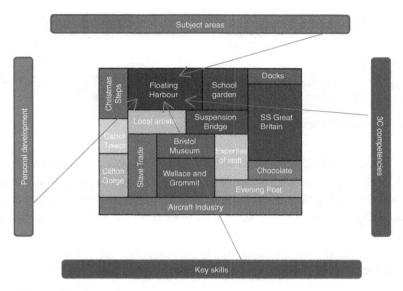

Figure 9.2 The floating harbour

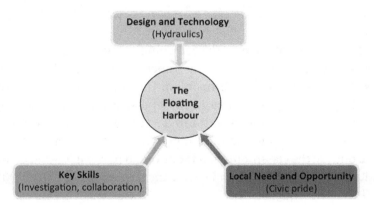

Figure 9.3 The harbour triangle

How can we get this going?

Many schools have used the Bristol method, and started with a list of local opportunities. Some have then matched these to their own local needs or aims, such as civic pride or widening horizons. These can then

Local Needs		Local Opportunities			
		Suspension Bridge	Slave Trade	Chocolate	SS Great Britain
	Civic Pride	X		X	X
	Inter-ethnic understanding		X	X	X
	Raised Aspirations	X	X	X	X

Figure 9.4 The local matrix

form a grid where local opportunities meet local needs (Figure 9.4). This might help clarify thoughts before the design stage. At this point, some of you will be saying that it's alright to talk about Bristol with its super-rich range of opportunities, but what about my town or village? You couldn't make much of a list here! However, it is surprising how much turns up in what starts off seeming a particularly barren patch for opportunities. You don't have to have a floating harbour and suspension bridge.

Learning outside the classroom

Many of these examples have involved going outside the classroom. Many schools became nervous about taking students out of school partly because they felt the pressure to 'get through' all the curriculum so did not have time, or they were worried about health and safety. Some schools still see going outside as a recreational extra to do after exams, and nothing to do with the curriculum. However, there is growing evidence that students learn far more outside the classroom than they ever do inside it. Ofsted confirmed this in its 2008 report, 'Learning Outside the Classroom' (ref. 0702190). This found that:

'Hands on' activities in a range of locations contributed much to improvements in:

- Achievement
- Standards
- Motivation
- Personal development
- Behaviour

The report tackled head-on the health and safety issue by finding that it actually improves students' safety by giving them experience outside the classroom. The key here is to teach students how to be safe in the 138 hours a week that they are not at school, and not just to keep them safe during the other 30 hours. The report states that: 'Experiences outside the classroom contributed significantly to "staying safe" '.

Part of the value in being outside the classroom comes from the added interest and engagement the students feel. Part of it is that the activities are more likely to be first-hand and practical. The experiences are often more memorable and:

- Memorable activities led to memorable learning.
- The place where activities happened often added to their value.

These experiences are most valuable when they are built into the overall curriculum rather than being seen as one-off experiences, and interestingly, secondary schools are sometimes better than primary schools at doing this:

- Primary schools are good at using their own grounds and the local area flexibly.
- Secondary schools are good at promoting high quality integrated learning on day and residential visits.

Harnessing the local community

The final part of locating national expectations in a local setting is the local community itself. This is often a resource that is not fully exploited in curriculum design.

Church Times
The local sixteenth-century church was part of the Year 8 programme where history, geography, D&T, English and religious education (RE) combined to base work around a visit and discussion with church officials. On this occasion the vicar was pointing

to the pressing need for repairs even though there was quite a lot of interest in the building as a historical monument. He also said that people were always asking for more information which was difficult to supply.

The students, all of whom lived nearby, but few of whom had ever been in the church, could see a commercial potential. What the church needed was a DVD and booklet that could be sold. A website could generate interest and solicit donations.

Because this was a joint project, the students were able to set about the task within English, history and ICT combined with RE. They interviewed both church officials and local people about the church and its role in their lives. They found out about the church, but also found out about their own community and learned to see its members as individuals. They listed the local people married there and videoed interviews about the way people saw it within their lives. Some remembered sheltering in the crypt during the war. All of this was woven into the DVD.

The DVD looked very professional and included music as well as a commentary and clips from the interviews. It sold well. The website became a community project with the students co-ordinating a wide range of contributions. Money was raised, interest generated and the students ended up feeling much more a part of the community than they ever had before.

We have talked about the opportunities that exist in the locality, and often the major resource is the local community itself. The contribution can come in unexpected ways, such as the Michelin starred restaurant in Chapter 2. We often think of local artists and writers or local business people when we invite people into school, recognizing that there is a wide range of people who have skills and knowledge from which we can learn. One issue for the school is knowing who is out there who might help. The much more important issue is making the help an integral part of the curriculum and not a one-off sideshow.

The involvement of employers is most successful when the employers' contribution is an integral part of the curriculum; When they meet with departments and work with them to identify opportunities to contribute; When they tailor that contribution to the syllabus, and provide practical contexts for specific learning. They turn up in school to contribute to specific lessons. They take students into their workplaces and set them specific tasks to do with items of learning specific to them. This is very different from coming along to school to give a talk, or to showing some students around the factory or office.

Student voice

We could not refer to the involvement of the wider community without taking account of the students themselves: an important part of that wider community, but also an important local community in themselves. Almost all the examples we have looked at so far have involved students having some degree of control of their own learning. They have developed ideas and selected lines of investigation. They have taken learning in directions that the teacher has not envisaged, and had been encouraged to do so. They have made some experiences last all term that were intended to last for a day.

Students learn from each other, and strengthen the process of their own learning by learning with others (Craft 2008). We often group students and ask them to work together, but we do not always design the curriculum specifically to suit this form of learning. But the value of students working together is not achieved without good design. There is evidence that friends working together are more likely to engage in exploratory talk (Barnes & Todd 1995, Mercer 2000) and complete tasks more effectively (Howe & Mercer 2007, Blatchford et al. 2008), and the composition of groups is important to the design of learning. Howe and Mercer also point to the need for curriculum design to create the experiences that require students to work together with specific roles, and not just do individual tasks while sitting together.

Student voice is sometimes seen in terms of a formal say about learning, usually at the beginning of a topic. There is often a session where students are told that next term's topic will be the Romans and are then asked what they already know, and what they would like to find out. The second question always seems particularly hard to answer. How can you know what you don't know? This is Donald Rumsfeld territory. If the students truly have a voice here, then there is a danger that whole areas of learning will be missed because students had no idea that they existed, so could not say that they would like to learn them.

Much more valuable is to give students an active role as learning develops, with the scope to direct and shape it. The more open-ended the learning situation, the more scope students have to direct it. The more formal and closed, the less chance they have. This also depends upon the teacher's flexibility and willingness to allow the learning to take a direction they had not considered. This willingness comes from a confidence that the key overall framework is not being distorted, but that learning is taking different pathways within this framework.

With some flexibility of approach and design, teachers can make use of all that a locality offers in terms of settings, resources and people. They can place learning in the local environment and community, meet local needs and take advantage of local opportunities. They can ensure that students go to the beach, commission statues, work in restaurants, explore the rich heritage of Bristol or work with the elderly people on their doorstep. And students can also work together and strengthen their learning in so doing.

In many schools, it is very difficult to achieve the flexibility to gain these benefits. Teachers say they would love to be able to vary the programme and take the students out of school and into practical situations. They would love to be able to give them more time on occasion to get into things in depth. Unfortunately, much as they would love to do all these things, they can never manage to do so. One thing stops them – the timetable.

But it doesn't need to stop good learning, and this is the subject of the next chapter.

10

The timetable

My Timetable; Your Timetable

Amrit is in Year 9 and is in the auditorium enjoying the fort-nightly mathematics lecture. Today it is a demonstration about geometry.

He watches a video about the use of the theoretical dimension in the design of road signs using distorted geometry. He engages in several conversations with student colleagues about the challenges that have been set by the teaching team. He makes notes as he wishes and there is no required work to be done.

As the session finishes he consults his planner to see the sessions that will follow this introduction. This extends through the next two weeks until the group meets again in the culmination of this unit.

Amrit is programmed for some practical workshops, some discussion sessions, two opportunities to work one-to-one with his mathematics teacher, and there is an expectation that he will follow, with necessary support, some units in a course textbook.

He is working on the early stages of his GCSE syllabus and is in the company of students in Years 10 and 11.

The unit is part of his individualized work plan, his curriculum. All the students have their own. Each student sits with their personal tutor and works out the next stage of their learning based on their enjoyment and success in recent stages and the progress they are making.

In English, maths and science, Amrit is sometimes taught in a group of 150 and sometimes in a group 20 or of 5. In other subjects, he stays with his year group for some of the time, but is sometime in mixed year groups.

> The school calls it the timetable, but sees it as 1,200 individual student timetables that coincide, rather than one school timetable that fragments. Amrit thinks this works for him.

How could the students in Chapter 2 spend all day in the restaurant? Or the students in Chapter 4 spend all day on the beach? What was happening to the timetable? What were all the other students doing? And what about the teachers who were with them? What was happening to the classes they were timetabled to teach?

Many schools talk about being 'off timetable' in these situations, or when they arrange a special technology challenge day, or arts week. However, these events have usually been arranged and planned in advance, and so, in a very real sense, they are an integral part of the timetable. This, of course, involves seeing the timetable as the schedule of learning experiences that has been arranged, rather than as the printed chart that sets out who is going to teach which class which subject in which room at what time.

A school timetable is more than this chart, because it embodies a model of the curriculum, and it structures how students will learn. The model or structure is usually implicit rather than explicit, and is not always discussed and agreed. The danger is that the 'timetabler' tends to perform whatever sort of magic they need to juggle all those subjects, rooms, teachers and teaching groups, taking account of options and examination schedules, and the rest of the school has to work with it, even though it does not always represent the model they really espouse. That is why schools have to 'come off timetable' or 'collapse the timetable' in order to achieve the model of learning that they want. So, before we look at timetables, it would be helpful to consider some models first – just as we might do in school!

Pressures on the timetable

Most secondary schools around the world use a version of a basic timetable model and apply variations to suit their needs. Being close to the model has certain strengths because the school is working with the implicit high standards associated with tradition. Moving away from the model can generate enthusiasm because the school would be 'ground-breaking', but too far from the model and the school can be seen as too much of a risk.

Everyone is used to a school system where all the students arrive at once, they are subdivided into teaching groups based on year of entry to the school, they visit or are visited by specialist teachers on five or six occasions during the day. Breaks and lunch are integrated. The students go home at the end of the day. They are given some work to do after lessons. As the size of secondary schools has grown, the basic model has been extended and adapted, but it is still recognizable as the basic model.

Why is this? Why have school timetables changed so little in their basic design over a century? Grocery retailing has changed beyond measure in recent years. Traditionally, shops opened for set hours and the experience was one of walking to a counter and being served by a specialist. Now supermarkets are open all hours, and customers serve themselves from the shelves. Similarly, cinemas used to show one film and customers queued to enter at the time set and all left at once. Now, cinemas show a range of films and welcome customers whenever they wish to arrive. And of course, most of us now shop on the internet and watch films at home on our own screens.

Could schools change as shops and cinemas have done? Could we become more flexible and personalize our offer? But would we want to make the timetable different simply to be different? Would we want to change it because there must be a way to beat the frustrations of historical tradition? Or are we looking for better ways of helping students gain the most benefit from the learning offer?

Some key questions

Before we can start drawing up a timetable we need to ask (and answer!) some key questions:

1. Is the curriculum to be arranged in subjects or in integrated blocks – or somewhere in between?
2. Is this to be the same for all year groups?

3. Will students always be grouped by year?
4. Are allocated sessions to be all the same length? If so, will they vary in multiples of the basic session (doubles, triples, etc.)? Or will there be a wide variety of lengths?
5. Is every week to be the same as every other through the year?
6. Will all days start and end at the same time? Will all breaks be taken at the same time?
7. Will all students and staff start and finish at the same time?
8. How will we deal with options?
9. Will options only be available at Years 10 and 11?

The answers to these questions will be based on the curriculum model (or models) that the school has in mind.

Curriculum models

In answer to the first two questions, there are a number of approaches. For Key Stage 3, the possibilities include those shown in the following table:

Subject or integrated
As Question 3 suggests, the model need not be the same for all year groups.

Model 1	Single subject approach
Model 2	Single subject plus some 'integrated' days or weeks
Model 3	Totally integrated
Model 4	Any combination of the above

Many schools now run an integrated approach in Year 7, or in Years 7 and 8, or even in Years 7, 8 and 9 as shown in the following table:

Variable by year group

Model 5	Integrated Year 7 followed by single subject Years 8 and 9
Model 6	Integrated Years 7 and 8 followed by single subject Year 8
Model 7	Integrated Years 7, 8 and 9

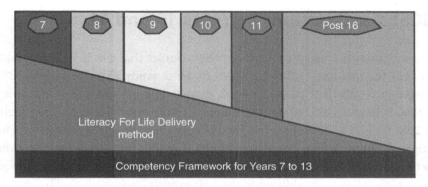

Figure 10.1 A tapering curriculum

A variation of this is the 'tapering' curriculum where some basic competencies are given progressively less time as they become established. In the example shown in Figure 10.1, the Literacy for Life course takes progressively less time, while the competency framework continues through the school.

Many schools are now offering students options during Key Stage 3. These are options outside the statutory curriculum. This is possible at Key Stage 3 because it is possible to cover the programmes of study in 2 years, so leaving space for options.

Including options

Model 8	Statutory curriculum: Monday–Thursday; options on Fridays
Model 9	Statutory curriculum: mornings and one afternoon; options on two afternoons
Model 10	Years 7 and 8 statutory curriculum; Year 9 options

The notion of options for Years 7–9 also takes account of the notion discussed in Chapter 1, that a national curriculum should not take up all of curriculum time, and that a school should be able to make its own unique contribution. This contribution might take the form of offering optional courses not in the usual national curriculum (photography, cooking, motor maintenance, etc.) or a particular course that the school runs for all students. Many people suggest that it is hard to do anything that has got nothing to do whatsoever with the national curriculum, and that photography could be part of art, and motor maintenance could be part of design and technology. However, there is often a sense of release in designing a course that does not have to conform to external requirements.

GCSEs and options in Years 10 and 11

These options are usually GCSE or other courses that can be taken in addition to the statutory subjects. Most students study eight or more GCSE courses or equivalent courses over 2 years. Some schools are now looking at this differently, and enabling students to study four GCSE or equivalents in Year 10, and another four in Year 11. This gives the opportunity to spend longer on subjects like English or Maths if grades need improvement, and so to continue studying them in Year 11. Some of these schools include an option in each year in addition to the four examination courses. This option could be a further GCSE or a non-examination course. Some students taking a non-examination option in Year 10 (such as cooking) turn it into a qualification in Year 11.

In these arrangements, there is no need for students of Years 10 and 11 to be taught separately, as courses are for 1 year only. However, most schools seem to do the compulsory subjects in Year 10 to give the opportunity for extension into Year 11.

When the new diplomas were introduced in England, they posed interesting question for the timetable as they incorporated a new curriculum model. Diploma students were required to spend time each week in a workplace setting provided by employers. The travel and logistics meant that this could not be done within the usual timetable, so two afternoons or a whole day had to be blocked in. However, not all students were doing the diploma, so it raised the question of what the rest of the year group would do during these blocks. Just carrying on with the normal curriculum was not an option because the diploma students would be missing it. Therefore, new courses were developed and run in the longer blocks. This had profound implications for the sort of learning that took place in these longer blocks, and the schools saw great improvements in learning which could be more practical, open-ended and challenging. Even though the diplomas are no longer supported by the government, many schools are still adhering to this model of learning. These sorts of models have clear implications for the timetable.

The variable day

There are many current variations on the variable day. Some schools are open from 7:00 in the morning until 7:00 at night, and run courses throughout the day. This does not mean that staff and students need to be there all the time; they come at appropriate times. This is a Further Education model that seems impossible at first, but many schools are running it successfully. It allows scarce resources and facilities to be spread more equitably, and allows students (and teachers) to opt for early or late starts. This extended timetable could work with any of the above models.

Another aspect of the variable day is to give flexibility over breaks. Instead of timetabling breaks, each teacher decides when a break should be taken. This usually happens in systems where there is something like three 2-hour blocks during the day. Teachers take a break whenever it is convenient during the block. The break in the middle block is for lunch; hence, sometimes this block is longer. Schools running this system say that it relieves pressure on the recreational space and the dining facilities as the whole school is not out at once. Classes make decisions about the best time, either based on the appropriate break for learning or on other considerations – it's no good going to lunch now, the canteen will be too crowded.

These sorts of arrangements also have significant implications for the timetable.

Length of sessions

We have already touched on this. Sessions could be of any length from 10 minutes to a week or more. The traditional session was based on Victorian notions that students' attention span was limited, and so lessons could not last for more than 30 or 40 minutes. As Victorian lessons tended to be rather boring, this was probably correct. However, in our much more exciting and engaging ways of learning, students will become absorbed by their more open-ended work and will not want to stop their investigation just as they are getting into it, so sessions can be much longer.

We talk about the reasons for different length sessions below, but here it is worth remembering that sessions need not be of a standard length across the week or year. Nor, if they vary, does the variation have to be in multiples of the standard session. This may have been necessary when the whole complexity of the timetable was worked out on squared paper, or later with Lego blocks, but now that we have computer programmes, we need not be so constrained; nor does every week have to be the same. You may be thinking that it is hard enough to remember where you are supposed to be at the moment, and you'd never remember at all if every week was different. Schools that run a 6-day revolving timetable have the same issue.

But giving a greater variety of session length should allow us to give an appropriate time for the learning that we are seeking to promote.

Considerations of design

So how do we decide which of these models to choose? The key to decisions about curriculum models and the timetable is the intended learning for the students. Some things might be best learned in a series of short-burst sessions. Other things might be best learned in extended sessions that could last a number of days. It might not be the case that one subject always needs short sessions while another needs longer ones. It could be that different parts of subjects have different needs in terms of time. In English primary schools, children traditionally are taught by the same teacher for all subjects, so the teacher can choose on a daily basis how long to allocate to each piece of learning. In most English secondary schools students are taught by a variety of teachers, and as they tend to be large institutions, there needs to be some structure for allocating this. But the structure does not have to be rigid, uniform and confining.

But how can we plan a timetable that allocates just the right amount of time – and at the right time – for learning? Some aspects of French may need a number of short sessions for practice each day – but maybe not every day of the year. Geography fieldwork may take a whole day, or 2 days, but this does not happen every week and other geography sessions might be better short.

So a key decision is always about the length of a session. We need something that is not too long for PE (or they would get too fatigued!) but long enough for art where you can't keep letting your paint dry and starting again next week. One solution is to allocate time in multiples of a session; singles for PE, doubles for science and triples for art. This gives some flexibility, but still does not allow for variations in need over the year. Nor does it allow the geography class to spend 2 days on a field trip in one week, but not in another.

So how can we get the flexibility we need to respond to differing and changing learning needs, while still retaining the structure that allows a large institution to function smoothly?

Timetable models

Where schools have responded innovatively to the recognition that varying the length of time needed for learning a particular aspect of a subject will vary throughout the year and even from day to day, they have tended to do so in three ways.

One way is to construct a timetable that has a wide variety of sessions of different lengths within it that can be allocated to different subjects to respond to needs. For example, in a notional 38-week year, 18 weeks can be divided into hour-long sessions, 10 weeks into whole-day sessions and 10 weeks into whole-week sessions (Figure 10.2). Subjects are then given an allocation of hours, days and a week. The different patterns are not usually in a block, but are spread through the year. This gives each subject a variety of time slots and they can plan their work accordingly, carrying out a field trip or a long investigation during the 1-week slot and short-burst work during the weeks with the 1-hour sessions.

A second way is to recalibrate the timetable through the year. When timetables were worked out and written by hand there was an understandable reluctance to change them during the year, but now that they can be done by computer it is possible to take stock of learning part way through the year and so take account of changing needs.

The third way is to give flexibility to staff to vary the timetable themselves. This may seem impossible, but it can be accomplished within a faculty system where Key Stage 3 students are taught by only five or six teachers, and where there are fewer sessions in a day with each session being longer. This gives the opportunity for teachers to come to 'local' agreements to swap,

Figure 10.2 Timetable variety

change or put sessions together. In Chapter 14, we give an example of a school where the set timetable was being ignored for almost 50 per cent of the time because teachers had found better solutions.

Flexibility is also achieved when longer sessions are allocated for integrated studies that combine subjects. With whole-day or whole-week sessions, teachers from different subjects can agree between them on the emphasis to be put on different aspects of learning.

Perhaps the best way of achieving flexibility is for teachers to tell the time-tabler what they need, rather than the timetabler telling them what they are going to get.

Dear Timetabler

Could each head of department analyse the programmes of study and determine what time is needed at different points in the programme, and then request the timetabler (Figure 10.3) to make it happen!

What this does is to put the planning where it needs to begin, with the learning and the students' needs, a bit like the provision made in the school that teaches Amrit at the start of the chapter. Schools that do it this way, set the timetabler a different problem. They start with the designing of the learning experiences they want to provide for students, and then ask the timetabler to help them with the provision of appropriate time, space and people.

Each department could similarly ask for support in managing what they see as the best way to make their subject successful (Figure 10.4).

If you are a timetabler, you may well be aghast on reading this. Isn't the timetabler's life difficult enough already! But the experience of the time-tabler in creating the time and space for better learning is always positive. After the initial trepidation, it is a matter of 'starting from a different place' and then making it work. The rewards when it does work are gratifying for everyone and most of all the students.

There is not one single model that is perfect for all schools. Like everything else in this book, it is a matter of thinking through the school's needs and devising the solution that best fits these. If you have already found a good solution, please post it on the companion website!

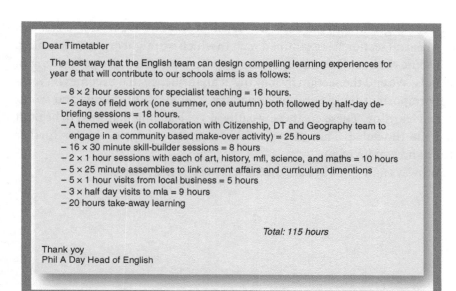

Dear Timetabler

The best way that the English team can design compelling learning experiences for year 8 that will contribute to our schools aims is as follows:

- 8 × 2 hour sessions for specialist teaching = 16 hours.
- 2 days of field work (one summer, one autumn) both followed by half-day de-briefing sessions = 18 hours.
- A themed week (in collaboration with Citizenship, DT and Geography team to engage in a community based make-over activity) = 25 hours
- 16 × 30 minute skill-builder sessions = 8 hours
- 2 × 1 hour sessions with each of art, history, mfl, science, and maths = 10 hours
- 5 × 25 minute assemblies to link current affairs and curriculum dimentions
- 5 × 1 hour visits from local business = 5 hours
- 3 × half day visits to mla = 9 hours
- 20 hours take-away learning

Total: 115 hours

Thank yoy
Phil A Day Head of English

Figure 10.3 Dear timetabler

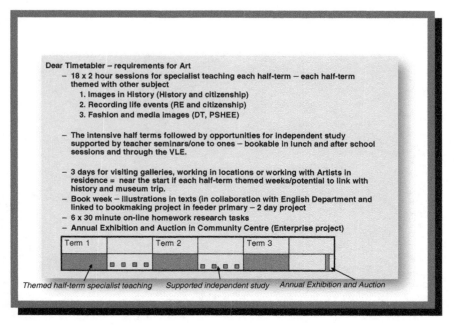

Dear Timetabler – requirements for Art
- 18 x 2 hour sessions for specialist teaching each half-term – each half-term themed with other subject
    1. Images in History (History and citizenship)
    2. Recording life events (RE and citizenship)
    3. Fashion and media images (DT, PSHEE)

- The intensive half terms followed by opportunities for independent study supported by teacher seminars/one to ones – bookable in lunch and after school sessions and through the VLE.

- 3 days for visiting galleries, working in locations or working with Artists in residence = near the start if each half-term themed weeks/potential to link with history and museum trip.
- Book week – illustrations in texts (in collaboration with English Department and linked to bookmaking project in feeder primary – 2 day project
- 6 x 30 minute on-line homework research tasks
- Annual Exhibition and Auction in Community Centre (Enterprise project)

Term 1		Term 2		Term 3	

Themed half-term specialist teaching   Supported independent study   Annual Exhibition and Auction

Figure 10.4 Art requirements

At the beginning of the book we looked at what we are trying to achieve. This central section has examined ways in which we might organize learning, and some of the influences upon the ways in which we manage learning in schools. We end the section by looking at an influence that becomes increasingly important by the end of secondary school: qualifications and work-related learning. These create new pathways of learning that need to be built into the timetable. They also provide students with gateways for further study and employment.

Pathways and gateways are the subjects of the next chapter.

11

Pathways and gateways

Engineering Better Mathematics

The engineering workshop was a busy place. Year 10 was focused on their practical work and highly motivated and engaged. There was no rush to leave at the end and there was clearly real interest in the extended projects that had been going on for several weeks.

What was interesting for the school was that this Year 10 group would not have been everyone's favourite class. Indeed, elsewhere in the school, some of the same students were known for their unwillingness to engage.

The curriculum leader for the school noticed the difference. The students were studying for a BTEC in engineering and what was interesting was that they did not seem to be phased by the mathematics, whereas mathematics lessons provided an example of the worst of their behaviour.

The mathematics team were invited to visit the engineering workshop to see what was happening. They watched, chatted with students, looked at the mathematics work and concluded that the element that made the real difference was that the mathematics was accepted by the students because of its application to what they saw as real situations. For this low ability group, the typical linear presentation of abstract mathematics was on a hiding to nothing.

The mathematics colleagues went back to their base and worked out how they would respond. It didn't take them long to decide that the best way forward would be to find opportunities within the engineering course for students to follow the GCSE maths course within a practical context. The two qualifications became merged to the benefit of both.

By the end of compulsory schooling at the age of 16, there is a natural focus on the courses, qualifications and experiences that young people need in order to move into the world of work, or on to the next stage of education. To prepare students at the age of 16, courses need to start at 14 or even earlier, and this is, quite rightly, a major influence on the curriculum for students in this age group. However, this does not mean that the principles of design that we have been talking about so far need to be abandoned. Qualifications provide pathways for learning and gateways to further learning and employment.

Nationally endorsed qualifications offer both recognition of someone's competence in a particular area, and also a framework of learning to achieve that competence. They provide a structure within which students can gain public recognition for their achievements and enable society to ensure that levels of competence are being maintained in the workplace. (At the simplest level it ensures that the person mending your tap knows how to do so.) The qualification entitles the holder to progress to higher levels of education or into certain areas of employment. So qualifications provide both a structure for learning, and also a public endorsement of that learning.

Of course, over the recent past, qualifications have also been used to give an indication of the relative successes of schools because they are publicly listed in 'performance tables'. Using the results in this way can distort the work of a school, because the leadership risks concentrating on a narrowing set of 'measures' rather than the aims established for the school.

The workplace can provide a rich context for learning. It can be a rich source for many of the features of 'irresistible learning' that we discussed in Chapter 8: at best it is authentic, worthwhile, engaging and motivating. Vocational qualifications, such as the BTEC engineering course in the above example, combine the features of workplace with the structure and endorsement of the qualification to the advantage of both.

The wide suite of qualifications that are available to schools enables a variety of pathways to be planned for students. Because there are so many qualifications, all with different demands, the problem is often seeing the wood for the trees so that an appropriate pathway can be planned.

The qualifications jungle

If the curriculum is a tree, then qualifications are a jungle.

In England, there are 144 recognized awarding organizations, and 9,708 accredited qualifications (Ofqual Annual Report 2010), with numbers rising! There are 539 GCEs, 691 GCSEs and 8,478 other qualifications. Despite efforts to reduce this, the number continues to go up. Awarding bodies are continuously adding to the mix, and new qualifications and revised ones are added each year. The largest numbers are in the 'other' category, which are mostly vocational or vocationally related (have a general application to work rather than being a specific qualification for one job). In a presentation to Ofqual's 'A new look at standards' conference on 13 October 2011, Cambridge Assessment identified 40 purposes and functions of qualifications, all of which make the jungle seem even more impenetrable. Yet we have to find pathways through this for our young people.

Attempts have been made to streamline these through the introduction of the Qualification Framework, (which classifies all qualifications in three key levels, with Level 1 equivalent to a GCSE pass at Grade D or below, Level 2 equivalent to a GCSE pass at Grade A*–C, and Level 3 equivalent to an 'A' Level pass), but although progress was made initially, this has stalled as government policy around vocational education and qualifications responds to the Wolf Report, 'A Review of Vocational Education' (Wolf 2011).

So how does a school make sense of all of these qualifications?

In the jungle, there are different classes of plants, and these divide into families and then further into species. So it is with qualifications. There are two main classes: academic or general qualifications and vocational or vocationally related. They have common characteristics such as the level they test, but may be substantially different in purpose or structure. Each of these classes subdivides into families – GCSEs, iGCSEs, NVQs (National Vocational Qualification), etc. These keep the characteristics of the class – they have a level attached to them and have specific common purposes. Below this are the individual qualifications within each family such as a GCSE subject. A further complication in the English system is that there is more than one

GCSE qualification for each subject. In fact, there are many varieties of the so-called Heinz model.

The use of qualifications to build a wide and enriching curriculum for young people can be distorted by the use of pass rates as a measure of a school's overall success. This can result in pressure on schools and students to select one pathway rather than another because of its impact on the school's results, rather than the student's learning. This is exacerbated by the attachment in England of higher value to an academic qualification over a vocational one. There may be a national table of equivalence between all the qualifications, but still in the minds of many people, including some employers and universities, the academic qualifications are seen as of higher value than vocational ones.

The introduction in England of the new Baccalaureate (E-Bacc) is also distorting the picture. The Baccalaureate is not actually an award for students, but a measure of schools' performance against a narrow range of GCSE subjects (English, maths, a foreign language, sciences and history or geography). This means that many schools will encourage students to take these subjects even though they may not be the most appropriate for the student and their choice of career or further education. Most other countries have some form of a baccalaureate, but these usually have a much wider set of expectations and give students an element of choice.

The selection of the right qualification pathways is a key component of curriculum design for students at the age of 14, but the principles of design remain the same. The best learning pathway is the one that is most likely to bring about the aims we set, and to provide the rich experiences that will allow a young person to achieve their potential.

In most cases, schools, together with the students themselves and their families, will work out the best qualification pathways for each individual. The danger is always that the pathway choice is influenced by external considerations such as those above. There are also institutional pressures such as facilities and timetables that can influence choices and can restrict options.

Some groups of schools get round some of the institutional pressures by making joint provision, especially across the less popular courses and qualifications. This means co-ordinating timetables and option blocks, and it means students travelling, but it does increase the options open and does help ensure that the pathway choices are made in the students' best interest.

Qualifications are an essential ingredient, so how do we determine the school's offer?

The principles are those we have set out through this book: the provision of a challenging, worthwhile and engaging curriculum that creates opportunities for progression, and maximizes the potential and talents of students. It is helpful to go back to the school's key aims and values in making these decisions. These might include:

- Learning comes first – the syllabus for qualifications should support and not drive the curriculum. This should apply not just in terms of content but in methodology and assessment. The qualification can be inspirational, aspirational and motivational if we select well and use it properly.

- Qualifications must open doors for learners, whether into further education, academic study or into employment. They must enable progression, so they need to be valued by those learners striving to achieve them.

- Qualification achievement should empower individuals. It should build self-confidence in the students, so the choice of qualification must be realistic in relation to the individual learner's potential for achievement and should not set them up for failure. Too often, students are allowed to select qualification entries which narrow rather than widen their career options.

- Qualifications need not distort the curriculum. Instead they can be used to enhance it.

So we need to ask ourselves, are the qualification pathways we construct the natural extension of the learning that takes place in the curriculum? Or are the examinations the educational equivalent of a chequered flag? There is no chequered flag in lifelong learning. Whichever way we see qualifications, students will be more successful if their learning makes sense to them and engages them.

Qualifications and design

In the opening example, BTEC engineering provided a practical context for GCSE maths as well as for its own learning. The course requirements of many qualifications often result in a widening of curriculum opportunities and enable learning to be put together in the holistic ways we have been discussing so far in this book. The English Diplomas are a good example of this, requiring workplace learning, functional skills, PLTS, as well as the core knowledge of the Diploma area of study. If you are familiar with the structure of the Diplomas, you will probably have already noticed that they are based on the 'tree'. The core learning is the leaves, and the functional skills and PLTS are the roots. The workplace provides the context, the 'trunk', where these are brought together.

The context of the workplace in learning can be immense. This could mean students spending part of their school time on work placements, or learning outside of the school in work environments, or it could mean replicating aspects of the workplace environment within the school. This could be physical aspects such as workshops or hairdressing salons – or it could be the disciplines and practices of the workplace. This is usually achieved most effectively by working closely with employers.

Vocational training

Employers traditionally hired young people and provided on-the-job training that brought the employability skills they needed. Expectations have risen and employers now argue that they expect this from schools. Recently the debate has been more intense with the promise of the Vocational Diploma qualification and the establishment of University Technical Colleges and Studio Schools as an attempt to restore an emphasis on vocational and practical learning.

The studio school brochure sets out what an approach might be for vocational and work-related learning for 14–19-year-olds. The vision is for schools to be rooted in their local community, to have close links with local employers. The curriculum is designed around the needs of learners and employers. The intention is to offer mainstream qualifications, within a personalized curriculum, that have the following features:

- Employability and enterprise
- Key qualifications
- Personalized curriculum
- Practical learning through project-based activities
- Real work experience – 2 days a week on work placement
- Access by students of any ability

Studio schools root the curriculum approach to learning and the overall experience in the real world, in partnerships with local and national employers.

In England, the model is new but it mirrors developing practice in other countries. In Canada and Australia, much progress has been made in structuring the curriculum and learning around virtual enterprise. There is no real work experience but a modelled workplace environment within simulated situations. The programmes' advantage over the real workplace is that it is possible to stop the clock in order to evaluate, reflect and improve. University technical colleges are emerging with similar ambitions of blending vocational learning with core national curriculum subjects.

What are the implications?

Teaching approaches need to support vocational approaches

The role of the teacher may need to differ from the traditional one. The Wolf Report (2011) suggested that teachers are not always sufficiently aware of the role they need to play in vocational learning. If the students' experience of work-related learning or vocational learning is to be effective, teachers have to be trained properly and be helped to understand the employment sectors and their needs. Most teachers have come straight through the education system themselves and have no experience of being in another sort of workplace. Schools might consider offering their staff real work experience themselves so that contexts add up in the classroom and they are able to adjust their role to make students' learning really effective.

Learning environments need to reflect the complexity of the work environment

Present day large secondary schools do bear some resemblance to modern work environments, but the overriding model for most rooms of learning is one where the students face towards a teacher's space. Of course there is need for this in some situations, but the image of most modern offices is open plan, with many computers and small meeting rooms. Similarly, the image of workshops is again one of ongoing busyness with occasional meetings. Schools have a balance to play between instruction and coaching and the old classroom model encourages one rather than the other. Work-related learning and vocational learning may perhaps require a greater emphasis on coaching.

Technology may need to be better utilized

In the world of work, computer technology is taken for granted. How we mirror this in schools is still an area of concern. Typically, though, in a modern work environment, projects are completed in groups whose members communicate with each other and use each others' knowledge, all using technology to the full. Of course, there are different sorts of 'work'; creative, entrepreneurial, craft, experimental, performance, fabrication and trade. All these lead to a range of economic and skill sectors which offer work and career prospects.

The curriculum therefore has to respond to this range of challenges. This whole section takes us back to Chapter 1 where we discussed what we are actually trying to achieve through our curriculum design. Educating young people to be good with their heads, hands and hearts means that all students will be expected to experience and see success and overcome problems in a range of learning challenges, including vocational and work-related learning.

Curriculum design at school level therefore needs to respond to these challenges and each teaching team, whether by department, faculty or otherwise, needs to offer learning that:

- exploits authentic tasks and problems,
- encourages some learner initiated and owned activity,
- expects teamwork,

- promotes skills such as negotiating, instructing and advertising,
- has real 'customers', sets deadlines and has quality standards.

Employer engagement is vital. Many schools have built strong partnerships over time and every community seems to have some form of business-to-schools liaison group. Of course, business has its own agenda of generating profit, which means that there is a limit to how much time they can commit to supporting schools. However, most need to demonstrate that they are exercising Corporate Social Responsibility, which they can do through their involvement with a school.

What business and industry need

In October 2011, the website for the Confederation of British Industry (CBI) stated:

> We look to our schools to prepare the UK's young people for the future and give them the skills and confidence to lead fulfilling and successful lives – that includes entering the world of work and developing productive and rewarding careers.

The CBI Report 'Fulfilling Potential' (2010), sets out a clear statement of business priorities for schools and the case for action. It makes it clear that employers do not expect schools to produce job-ready employees by the time they leave secondary school. What they do expect is to be able to recruit young people with the right skills, capabilities and attitude for the work place. They see these as:

- Good literacy and communication skills, including the use of IT.
- A broad set of so-called employability skills. That is, being able to work in a team, to solve problems, to communicate effectively, to understand how businesses work and the ability to self-manage their time.
- A strong grounding in science and maths, particularly numeracy skills.
- Access to a range of further learning options, whether academic, vocational or applied qualifications that are recognized, understood and valued by business.

Don Tapscott (1998) in his book *Grown up Digital* argues for ditching the Industrial Age model. This generation will need to learn in different ways and it is not what you know but how you learn that matters. Even employers themselves cannot predict what will be needed in knowledge terms in the next decade or so. Tapscott argues that the employers' input is important for providing context, but more importantly for making young people aware of what he calls the 'know how': how to access information, how to use information and how to adapt to change.

Since the late 1980s business has been expected to be represented on governing bodies of schools, and business engagement is growing, and more and more employers want a say, and to exert yet more influence on the young people they receive at the end of the schooling process. This accounts for the rise in the number of schools and chains of schools being sponsored, either as academies or trusts, by business concerns. Business also sets out to influence central government by setting agendas within which the curriculum is framed. Sometimes the agenda is set through manipulation of the qualification system, which in turn affects the learning route of students, but more and more businesses, employers and professional bodies are providing internships, placements and work experience opportunities.

Curriculum design needs to ensure that these links and contexts are used most valuably in constructing learning experiences for the students. And it must not be forgotten that many students are experiencing the world of work anyway, in their own time and without the assistance of the school.

So how can we make work-related and vocational learning have an impact on the curriculum?

Schools are required to offer formal careers 'Information, Advice and Guidance', but the quality can vary significantly from school to school. The best provision in work related learning and vocational courses occurs when aspects of work and careers are included in the learning offer from the very beginning. Whatever the organization of the learning, whether it is in subject departments, faculties, or other teams, we need to ensure that there is reference to the real world and the world of work in all aspects of teaching.

Whatever the age of the learners, whatever the subject, theme or project: students need to understand the application of what they are learning to the world of work.

A science department might have a display of all the jobs that science can take us towards. From radiologists, to paramedics, to water board technicians, to marine archaeologists, students need images of jobs. Every subject discipline team could be asked to spend a short time on a training day, looking at where the essential elements of their subject discipline lead to in the world of work. Many are surprised by how hard teachers find this. For the reasons mentioned earlier in this chapter, teachers' own previous experienc,and the focus on syllabus and examinations mean that many teachers have little time to consider where it all leads.

Figure 11.1 provides an example from the arts. Starting with the subject in the centre, place a few key words around it and then extend outwards into the jobs available. Whatever the subject, journalism will be one of the possibilities. What a message that might be for the students and for the English team!

The challenge after the initial few minutes of building the chart is to keep emphasizing the possibilities and keep the students thinking about the world beyond school. This should not be in a career planning way but in a way which widens their understanding and keeps them thinking about new possibilities.

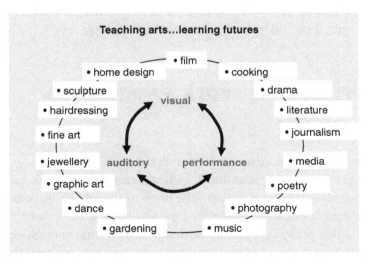

Figure 11.1 Learning futures

In Chapter 3, we talked about the whole picture of learning with the various elements 'carrying' the curriculum. In learning about work, schools employ a range of experiences beyond lessons. The well regarded Young Enterprise Scheme brings young people together to work with a mentor business person who helps them to make sense of the world of business finance as they compete with other schools locally to be most profitable.

The organisation 'Head Teachers and Industry' runs kite mark schemes for schools to encourage a focus on the skill sets that employers continuously argue are vital for our workforce. The 'Go for it' scheme promotes adventure and controlled risk taking as a means of developing entrepreneurial outlooks. The more recent 'Inspire' scheme is aimed at those students at risk of becoming NEET.

Work experience

Work experience is described by many students as a turning point in their schooling. In Year 10, their two weeks attached to a well prepared employer shows them why their success at school is important. Of course, this depends upon well-managed and well-prepared work experience. The Wolf Report is critical of the present arrangements for work experience and recommends it moves away from the traditional Year 10 slot, arguing that because the age of participation is being raised, students will undertake work experience anyway at a later stage. However, schools might think that, if work experience can be a spur, it should be used earlier rather than later.

When should work experience take place?

Does it have to take place for all of Year 10 in June?

There are many historical and logistical reasons why work experience takes place after the exam season, just prior to the end of the school year, when the timetable can be abandoned for Key Stage 4 and other things can happen. Is this really best for the students? Just finding enough employers is a challenge and who could blame them if, in their wish to help, they overstretch in their ability to support effectively?

What if work experience was built into the schedule in a more flexible way and those students who were engaged in it had a chance to follow up by informing their peers about their experience? Over the course of a year, 30 different groups could be out at different times, but what stops this happening is that timetable problem. But the timetable is supposed to facilitate learning, not restrict it – as we discussed in Chapter 10.

Does all work experience have to be individual?

From being in a class group to suddenly being on one's own is a massive confidence shift for some young people. Can they engage in work experience in pairs or threes? Employers like this too.

Should work experience in other schools be excluded from the offer?

Many students who have little idea of where they want to be eventually select the 'working with young children' option as a way of solving an immediate problem, rather than as a conscious choice. They return to the familiar, often going to work in their previous primary school where staff remember them with affection or otherwise and not a little embarrassment. It might not be the step on the road to adulthood we might seek. If they do want to work in a school as teachers, it might be all the more reason to take work experience elsewhere. Otherwise we risk compounding one of the problems mentioned previously in this chapter: the teacher's lack of knowledge of the world of work.

How can we get students into small and medium sized businesses?

Small- or medium-sized enterprises (SMEs) are by far the largest job sector in England. Yet, these are the very businesses that have most difficulty in taking people on work experience. They run with the minimum of staff, with everyone fully committed to keeping it going and cutting costs, so there is little space for including another activity such as mentoring a school student. Some schools have begun to build relationships with local SMEs, and these have brought fruit over time.

Some other ways to build understanding of the world of work

Follow the training, job or career pathways of ex students

Many schools emphasize the achievements of ex students, some of whom are now local celebrities. This is fine and portrays the school in a good light, but aspiration is more than this. Just knowing that someone made it to the top in professional football only does so much in encouraging young people to think they can achieve. To get students to see pathways is a vital aspect of aspiration. School magazines might carry a pen portrait of an ex student with a description of their learning pathway since they said farewell. Ex students who feature in local newspapers (preferably for positive reasons!) might be celebrated and invited in to talk with current cohorts.

Some schools have a list of ex students who have volunteered to contact present students to talk about their experiences both at school and since. Much of this is about convincing students that GCSEs are not the chequered flag but the starting pistol.

An A–Z of jobs you never heard of: An online resource of short video clips, showing jobs you didn't know about and what they involve. This is done in an informal way and backed up by details of these jobs and how to find out more about them. There are some amazing web-based products available at present that help students to get into the mesh that is the world of work.

A day in the life of: Some schools build a local industry website – with videos of people in different jobs. Students log on to a website and see what a plumber/nurse/chef/barrister/florist/nursery nurse/bus conductor is doing at the time. This is backed up by further resources and information about the job and linked to the A–Z of jobs. This is a good way to get local SMEs involved . . . and students can do the filming and website work as part of their ICT course!

City exchanges: Schools twin up to present information about their local area to students from a different area. The link might explore culture, curriculum subject disciplines . . . and jobs. This can incorporate the contributions of local employers showcasing what they do.

Exploiting part-time work

A significant proportion of teenagers now have part-time work in the evenings, weekends and holidays, Some have significant responsibilities. In catering, for example, a school student can be part of a team that manages customers, deals with food hygiene and preparation, premises management, health and safety, money and security. Could we use the experience that students are gaining in their part-time work? Is the curriculum building on the wide range of skills that many students are developing outside of school? Is the work experience that we offer providing lower levels of responsibility than the students already have in their part-time work? The example below shows how extensive this can be:

Pink Strings

The conference interval begins and people enjoy refreshments as they are entertained by a string quartet of teenagers from a local school. Due applause follows and delegates return to the auditorium.

The quartet are all students at the local comprehensive, and are available for booking under their performance name, 'Pink Strings' (they all wear pink). They do weddings and other occasions, as it says on the flier they produce. They explain that a wedding will always generate more custom. Depending on the number of guests, they can predict the number of enquiries and bookings they will receive. They know the pattern for wedding bookings through the year, and in the quieter period at the end of November, they take their skills to York as buskers.

Their outlay on the train fare can be recouped in the first 30 minutes. Thereafter it is profit, except for the cost of lunch. They

---

start at 10 a.m., stop for lunch and go home when they have earned their target, which is usually around 3 p.m. They have a product analysis that tells them that: Typically, older people give less, younger give more. Few younger people are around early so slower music before lunch needs to be changed to faster tunes afterwards. Their profit level is surprising – and so are the business acumen and experience of these young musicians.

Pathways

We started this chapter by looking at how BTEC engineering could provide a practical context for GCSE maths as well as introducing young people into the practices and disciplines of the workplace. Both the qualification and the workplace experience enhance the curriculum by providing pathways for learning. Around the world, various diplomas and baccalaureates also enhance the curriculum, by providing pathways that combine workplace learning, functional skills, personal and social skills as well as the core knowledge of subject disciplines. This is our basic 'tree' model of curriculum design. The core learning is the branches of knowledge and the roots are those lifelong qualities that are learned and sustained through experience. The workplace provides the context (the 'trunk') where these are brought together.

Gateways

The qualifications also act as gateways to employment or further education, and to do this an assessment needs to be made of the students' learning. Assessment is the subject of the next chapter.

SECTION III

How will we know
if we are successful?

12 Assessment and evaluation

A Work Skills Passport

Conscious that employers were complaining that young people left school without being ready to be employed, a group of schools worked with local firms to identify the 'work readiness' skills and qualities that employers thought were necessary. They extended the search by asking former students who had recently found jobs what they could have learned at school that would have made work easier.

From these discussions the schools agreed on a list of 'work readiness' skills that bore a remarkable similarity to the list in Chapter 2. It included teamwork, problem solving, good communication, showing initiative, persistence and the 3Cs. These were broken down into elements that could be demonstrated. These are essentially the roots of the tree. Everyone bought into the list: employers had helped draw it up; parents were happy because it had employers' endorsement; schools could see they were important. Even students could see the point!

They turned this list into a Skills Passport for each student. This not only listed the skills, but set out lines of development for each. As the skills might be developed in any subject, it was the students' responsibility to identify when skills were being gained and implemented, and then to check their perception against that of the teacher concerned, and to obtain 'endorsement'.

At the end of each half term, the employers came into school to set a series of group tasks where students had to work together in teams to solve problems. The tasks were calculated to give participants the opportunity to display the skills on the passport.

This then became a chance for the employers to take part in the endorsement process.

When students applied for jobs, the skills passport became part of their portfolio, and as the local employers had been instrumental in setting it up and had endorsed the assessments, it became a passport to work.

The three key curriculum design questions have been:

1. What are we trying to achieve in terms of students' learning?
2. How should we organize learning to achieve this?
3. How will we know whether we have been successful?

The short answer to the third question is, 'We will know we are successful if the students have learned all the things we wanted them to learn'. The long answer is about how we find that out.

Before we look at that longer answer, we need to distinguish between the two implications of the question, 'Have we been successful?' The answer hinges around whether or not the students have learned the things we intended, but one aspect is about how successful the students have been in learning, and the other aspects is about how successful our curriculum has been in promoting that learning. The first aspect is Assessment, the second is Evaluation, and the two are closely linked. You might think that if the students did not learn what we intended, then the curriculum certainly wasn't successful, and vice versa. And you would be right. But there are, of course, grey areas where some students learn some things but not all, and so some bits of the curriculum might be better than others. We shall take the two aspects separately.

The importance of assessment

If we don't know what students have learned already, we cannot know what they need to learn next. If we don't know what they have failed to grasp, we cannot know where they need help or support. If we have no overview of how the class is doing, we cannot shape the curriculum around their needs.

But, if we have set ourselves (or the students) a wider set of goals, then we need to take account of this wider set when we seek to find out how successful we (or the students) have been in achieving them. We have nationally set levels for the national curriculum subjects and marking schemes for GCSE syllabi, but we have aims in the wider areas of personal development, key skills and the 3Cs. If we really think these are important, then we would be interested to know how our students are doing in these terms as well.

UNESCO sees four levels to the curriculum (Rychen & Tiana 2004):

1. The legislated or official curriculum (the one governments require).
2. The implemented curriculum (the one that schools actually teach, which is the school's interpretation of the legislated one).
3. The effective or achieved curriculum (the things students actually learn, which differs from student to student).
4. The assessed curriculum (those aspects of the above that are assessed).

In almost all cases, the assessed curriculum is much narrower than the legislated one. This has the effect of narrowing, in turn, the implemented one because schools tend to focus on what is important for examinations. (What you test is what you get!) So if we are serious about a broader curriculum, then we need to ensure that we have systems for assessing across that breadth.

Are all these things possible? Will we need to spend all our time assessing and have no time left for teaching? Can we actually make use of the assessment information we acquire?

Building assessment into design

Teachers spend much of their time trying to find out what their students know and understand. How many times in each lesson do teachers ask questions, not because they want to find out the answer, but because they want to find out who else knows the answer, too? This is all part of the process of finding out, but it is not always done in relation to the goals we originally set.

There are, of course, four key reasons why we want to find out what a student has learned:

1. To make a summative judgement about the student's achievement for reporting purposes.
2. To help evaluate the efficacy of the school and its curriculum.
3. To decide what the student should learn next.
4. To find out why they didn't learn what we expected.

These forms of assessment are generally called summative, evaluative, formative and diagnostic, respectively. In this chapter, we shall focus mainly on the implications of the third question. It is also essential to be able to evaluate the efficacy of the curriculum, so we shall look at this separately at the end of the chapter.

Assessment and curriculum design

There is a critical difference. Assessment is finding out what a student has learned from an experience. Curriculum design is ensuring that the experience will bring about the intended learning. Both processes have to be clear about what the intended learning is: assessment in order to look for it, design in order to bring it about.

Formative assessment – only half the information we need

The process of assessment involves finding out what students know, understand and can do. This is useful information, but not sufficient in itself for curriculum design. Because if it is to be useful in curriculum design, then we also need to know what it is that students don't know, can't do and don't understand. Because it is this that tells us what they need to learn next.

Even if you know exactly what a student knows, understands and can do, you do not necessarily know what they need to learn next. For example, if you were told that a Year 10 maths student knew how to calculate proportional change, use symbols to the nth term, and solve simultaneous linear equations in two variables, would you know what they should learn next? What do you think it should be: Calculate disproportional change? Use symbols to the $n + x$th term? Solve simultaneous linear equations in three variables? Be honest, maths teachers, do you know what comes next?

So, you can see that what a pupil should learn next is dependent not only on what they have learned already, but also on what they are *expected* to learn next. How do we decide what this is?

The example above was taken from the Level 7 Level Description for Number and Algebra in the English National Curriculum (QCA 2007a,b). So we could look at Level 8 to get some guidance on what to do next. (Multiply two linear expressions, solve inequalities in two variables, and sketch and interpret graphs of quadratic, cubic and reciprocal function – if you are interested. Or perhaps you already knew that!)

Of course, maths teachers do already know what it is that students need to learn next in maths, but that is because they are familiar with the set syllabus for England. If they were in a different country, the syllabus might well be set out in a different sequence. This is particularly true for subjects other than maths, which is more linear and has more universality across countries than other subjects. The point being made is that progress seen in this way is in terms of a syllabus or programme of study. Someone has set out a sequence of learning, the textbooks have been developed in terms of this sequence and so we know what is to be learned next.

This seems fairly straightforward. Once you know how to calculate proportional change, then you need to learn how to multiply two linear expressions. Whichever subject you are teaching, you just check the syllabus or programme to find out what comes next. Then, once your students have learned one thing, you move on to the next.

However, we all know that it is not quite as easy as that. First, what do you do when some students have learned to calculate proportional change, but others have not? Secondly, are there not *degrees* of learning within a topic or aspect? Thirdly, are all subjects quite as linear as this example from maths would suggest?

Assessment within an aspect of a subject

The answers to all the three questions above lie in looking at the progression of learning within any given subject, aspect or topic. The English National Curriculum level descriptions are probably more helpful here than we generally think. The geography descriptions are a good example. If we look at the elements that refer to places, we find:

- Level 2 – to *describe* the places they visit
- Level 3 – to make *comparisons* and *contrasts* between one place and another
- Level 4 – to begin to *recognize patterns* and make *generalizations*
- Level 5 – to give *geographical explanations* for those patterns
- Level 6 – to take account of *different sources* of evidence
- Level 7 – to *explain relationships* between causes

These are criteria that apply to any topic within geography. Whether students are engaged in a fieldwork study of a local village or the analysis of another country, they could be working at one of the above levels. These are intellectual levels that are concerned with the ways in which students *process* the knowledge they are acquiring. In turn the way they are processing extends and deepens that knowledge. Even though the whole class has moved on to the next topic, students within the class can be making progress within their levels of intellectual development.

The implications for teaching are significant. After a village study, the teacher would ask a series of questions to different students:

1. Tell us what the village was like.
2. How is that different from where we live? Is anything the same?
3. Have you noticed something about all the villages we looked at? Think of those on the hills and those by the river.
4. Why do you think that was?

You will have spotted that the questions address the different levels. The first asks for a description, so is Level 2. The second asks for a comparison, so is Level 3. The third is looking for a generalization (Villages on the hill are tightly packed, those by the river are spread out), so is Level 4, and the fifth is looking for an explanation for that relationship, so is Level 5. Of course, the questions are seeking to push students to the next level, not just keep them at the present one.

The other interesting point about these questions is that they have a double function. One function is to stimulate students' intellectual development: a teaching function. The other function is to ascertain the intellectual level at which the students are working: an assessment function. Assessment does not have to be a separate function from teaching. We do not have to teach something and then have a test to find out whether students have learned it. The everyday dialogue of teaching and learning is doing both.

Teachers do this naturally, and then worry needlessly about personalization. Personalization does not have to be about students undertaking different topics within the syllabus, but about working towards the next intellectual level within a topic.

The implications of the intellectual levels for *curriculum design* are profound, and in the longer term impact more generally on the nature of the experience chosen. For example, if you were targeting students who were still learning to make cogent descriptions of places, how many villages would they have to visit in order to write a description? Yes, just one would do. But how many would they need to visit in order to make contrasts and comparisons? At least two, and those villages would need some features in common and some different. The art of the curriculum designer lies in selecting villages that make this sufficiently obvious to the young geographer.

And finally, how many villages would students have to visit before they spotted that the ones on top of the hills had the houses packed closely together, while those by the river were spread out linearly? They would probably have to go to so many that there would not be sufficient time. So the curriculum designer needs to build other resources into the experience. The students would need to look at maps and pictures, or maybe aerial photographs or videos. At this level of learning, first-hand experiences would not be enough, and secondary sources would be necessary.

The key is that the experience is designed to achieve the *level* of learning that is appropriate for these students. This is raised as an issue not because Levels are important in themselves, but because they help us structure learning with increasing challenge. To make comparisons and contrasts is an intellectual level above writing a description, and to make a generalisation is a further level. This is also following Bloom's taxonomy of progressively deeper learning. This is not Levels for the sake of Levels, but the ensuring of intellectual challenge and deep learning.

Progressively deep learning

The same process can be applied to other subjects. For example, the sequence in history is:

- Level 3 – recognize *characteristic features* of periods they have studied
- Level 4 – recognize *changes* within and between periods
- Level 5 – to give *historical explanations* for those changes
- Level 6 – begin to *explain relationships* between causes
- Level 7 – *analyse causation* in a wide context

These steps help in the processes of design and assessment. Again, this is not just to push students to a higher level for the sake of statistics, but because it drives learning to a deeper level. In Bloom's taxonomy, knowing characteristic features of a period (the Egyptians built pyramids, the Victorians expanded the Empire) would be at the lowest or most superficial level of learning. When students recognize the reasons why things changed, they begin to comprehend more about history. This is Bloom's second level. To explain the relationships between causes and analysing causation takes students to progressively deeper levels of analysis and synthesis.

The Levels also demand a much greater knowledge base. To recognize the significance of changes between periods, and to give explanations for those changes, requires knowledge of several periods. To explain the relationships between causes requires detailed knowledge across a range of periods in history. These intellectual skills of explanation and analysis cannot be deployed in a vacuum. They need progressively deeper and more extensive knowledge.

There is also a key implication in these levels for both teaching and curriculum design. When students are expected to give explanations for changes, the implication is that they should be able to come up with these explanations from their knowledge of the periods in question. Not that they have been given some explanations and asked to remember them for a test.

What about the generic skills and competencies?

You might think that all this about assessing students' progress in subjects is what you do anyway. It is what subject specialists are good at. The real challenge is in the wider goals of the curriculum. What do we do here? In the earlier chapters we have spoken about:

- Personal development
- Key skills
- The 3Cs
- Subject areas

If we are to take these seriously, they all come together to form a framework of expectations that are wider than the subject areas (Figure 12.1).

This is the sort of framework that was drawn up in the 'work skills passport' in the opening scenario. In a sense it is just a list of expectations, but put into some sort of order or structure that makes it a 'framework'. The work skills passport included personal qualities as well as competencies such as problem solving and teamwork, and the 3Cs (the employers are interested in communication and basic calculation, rather than GCSE passes in English and maths). These were pulled out into lines of development that

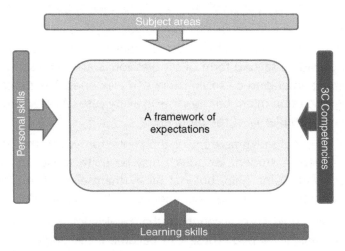

Figure 12.1 A framework of expectations

were relevant to courses that these students were following, and gave a perspective of development and progress.

Many schools have found it helpful to have such lists, and even more helpful if the lists are structured into frameworks that fit with the curriculum of the school. There is not just one way of doing this that every school should adopt. The best systems are those worked out by schools or groups of schools that are relevant to their own situations. In the scenario, the involvement of employers became a key factor in the success and credibility of the passport in the eyes of students and their parents. It also helped to gain the sign-up of staff.

The complexity of skills

Around the country, there are countless 'skills ladders' and numerous skills progression routes have been charted and are in use. We referred to these in Chapter 7. These are similar to the national curriculum level descriptions, breaking down the skills into steps and setting them out in levels. But there are other ways in which skills develop.

If we take one skill like problem solving, we could look at it in four ways:

1. First, we could take the skills-ladder approach and pull the skill out into steps or stages. These might be, in ascending order: identify problems, isolate factors, take account of multiple factors, suggest solutions, test solutions, etc.

2. Secondly, we could look at the sort of problems that need to be solved. These provide a second form of progression: starting by solving simple problems and ending by solving very complex ones. The procedure for finding a solution might be the same in every case. What changes is the increasing complexity of the problems.

3. Thirdly, we could take account of the context in which the problem is being solved. A student (or adult!) may be quite capable of solving a problem with some help, but not all by themselves. The progression might be one of increasing independence in the use of a skill.

4. Finally, we could take account of the knowledge contexts in which the skills are developed. These can become increasingly complex and extensive.

The first approach here is a good illustration of why many people are suspicious of skills ladders. They argue that breaking a skill down into its component parts may seem logical, but they are not learned like that nor are they used like that. Skills are developed and used holistically and not as separate parts.

A subject example from the English National Curriculum would be the Level 4 science expectation to control variables in an experiment. If the experiment involves rolling two cars down a slope, then it is fairly easy to control the variables, and most 11-year-olds can do it. If the experiment is to find the Higgs Boson in the Hadron Collider, then there will be few people in the world able to exert such control. It is not the ladder of the skill that needs extending to take account of this – it is the sheer extent and complexity of the experiment. This is why Hirsch (1987) argues that skills cannot exist outside a knowledge context.

The Hadron Collider also illustrates the fact that skills are often used within a team, rather than individually. There may be no one in the world with the skill to run that experiment all by themselves. It is only by working as a team that it can be done.

It is possible to put together the two dimensions of complexity and independence as vertical and horizontal axes, to form a matrix of progress (see Figure 12.2).

The line of progress here is from solving simple problems with some help to solving more complex ones independently. But the line of progress is

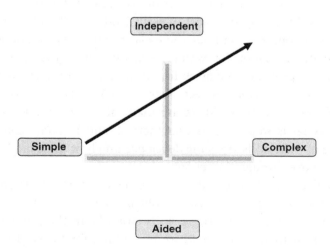

Figure 12.2 A matrix of progress

seldom as straight as the one depicted here. A student may become independent in simple situations, but still need help in more complex ones, so the line of progress may zigzag at first. Some of us may even continue to zigzag through life.

The impact of context is seen across the range of skills and attributes.

A range of contexts for skills

It might not even be the increasing complexity of the problems that is the mark of progress. It could be the range of problems that is important. To be better at a skill is to be able to perform it in an increasingly diverse range of situations. A student may be able to work well in a football team, but not when the team is engaged in science. Another student is creative in music, but not in D&T. It may be even more specific that that: being able to perform a skill in one aspect of a subject but not another. Not because they are more complex, but because they are different. Progression would therefore be seen as a greater range of performance.

A range of approaches

Schools have come up with many ways of assessing in the areas of skills and competencies. Most use some sort of skills ladder, while others add in the dimensions of contexts. Without some clarity about expectations there is likely to be little progress. For example, schools will say that they are developing students' problem-solving skills, but would not have worked out how these skills might develop between Year 7 and Year 11. Schools can either use an off-the-web solution (there are many about) or develop their own approach. What is important is that there should be some coherent and overall idea of what skills are being developed and how these might progress as students move through the school.

There is also a need to consider how any element of a skills progression would apply in different subjects. Is problem solving in maths the same as in art or D&T? What would these skills look like in the different subject areas, and from that, what would we be looking for to see if progress is being made?

Making it manageable

The danger of too extensive a structure of expectations is that they all get built into curriculum design so that it gets overloaded. Teachers try to cope with the overload by teaching more directly and giving students less time to explore ideas and practise skills. This results in students being stuck at Bloom's first level, rather than progressing to deeper levels. The interesting thing is that if a smaller key range of expectations was selected, and the students were given more time to develop skills within these contexts, they are likely to explore these other expectations anyway. The work of Charles Desforges (2002) is illuminating here. In seeking to map learning, he found that students frequently learned things not on the 'agenda' at all. Sometimes the learning was 'unlocked' by the learning of a new concept in a seemingly unrelated area. This is because learning is not the simple linear progression of our curriculum plans, but a more complex interrelated network of progression where one thing leads to a variety of others.

It is therefore important that when schools draw up any 'framework of expectations', they avoid the temptation to put in as much as they possibly can. If it becomes too long and detailed, it will cease to be a useful framework that guides learning even deeper, and will become instead an obstacle course of ground to be covered and hoops to jump through that actually impedes progress.

Implications for curriculum design

We looked earlier in this chapter at how increasing expectations of students' intellectual development impacted on curriculum design. The learning experiences that we design for students depend upon the precise learning that we are hoping to achieve. If we want students to learn to compare and contrast, they will need a different experience than if they were learning to make generalizations.

The same is true of the skills and competencies. Once we have a clear set of expectations for skills such as problem solving, then we can begin to design the sort of experiences that students need in order to learn them. So the set of expectations is not just a tool for assessment, it is a tool for curriculum design.

The passport for assessment becomes a passport to learning.

Co-operation across the school

If we are looking at skills and competencies that might be developed in a range of subject areas, then there needs to be co-operation between subject departments to ensure that progress is being captured, and that progress in one subject can be built upon in another. The skills passport in the opening scenario is one example of how this can be done. The onus was put on the student to provide the liaison between the departments. You may think that the school itself has a professional responsibility here, and that it should not be left entirely to students. Teachers could fill in their assessment of the students in terms of the skills or competencies. Either way, there is a need for someone within the school to keep the overview across the subjects, and ask the key questions about why is science saying that student X is an excellent problem solver when geography says they are poor? In Chapter 7, we suggested that a deputy head or head of year might keep the overview of competency development across the school or year, but unless the school was very small, one person is unlikely to be able to monitor individual progress in different subjects.

One method used by schools is the periodic student review in which the year group teachers get together to review overall progress. In a tutor-group system this gives a clear role to the tutor who becomes the co-ordinator of cross-department assessments. This becomes a key role in the co-ordination of skills and competency assessments and the tutor can ask the key questions. At the moment, the role of the tutor is often mainly pastoral; this brings it into the academic.

Has the curriculum been successful?

The key assessment question is whether the students have been successful in learning what was intended. The key evaluation question is whether we have been successful in designing a curriculum that has enabled them to learn those things.

The key concern about any curriculum change is how the school can be sure that at the end of the whole process all the new learning experiences

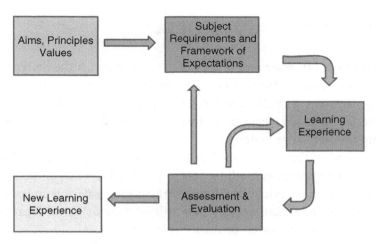

Figure 12.3 The evaluation process

will add up to a coherent, worthwhile, broad and balanced set of learning that will achieve the aims originally set. And we don't really want to wait until the end of five years and find that the GCSE scores have plummeted. We don't just need quality control, we need quality assurance.

Of course, assessment is both formative and summative, and so we do not have to wait until the end of the process to see if it is successful; we can check as we go along. In addition to the subject assessments we are making in terms of the national curriculum or syllabus, we have added the element of the 'framework of expectations' for the skills and competencies. These combine in a process set out in the model in Figure 12.3.

In this model, the information gained from assessments and evaluations inform three parts of the process:

1. The design of the next learning experience will be based upon what the students have learned in the present one.

2. The present learning experience may be amended as it goes along in the light of ongoing assessment. Or it may be decided to amend it before using it again, or never to use it again.

3. There might be implications for the school's framework of expectations itself. It might have been too ambitious, or not ambitious enough. Or the framework might need amending for a particular class or group that had needs different from the usual.

Keeping the overview

In terms of quality assurance it is essential to impact on the designs *before* they are carried out to help ensure that they are appropriate to the intended learning. In terms of quality control, it is important to review the *outcome* of the experiences to see what was and was not learned and how this needs to feed into the next stage of design.

The second of these helps the 'feedback loops' in Figure 12.3. The subject teacher or department will be able to provide feedback to facilitate the design of the next experience, and amend the present one; but amending the framework for the school or next class will be done between departments. Here is where the tutor or co-ordinator role comes in.

If the students achieve the expectations of the subject and of the framework, then the curriculum will have been successful in promoting its aims. And if the framework is broad and coherent, then the curriculum will be so too, so long as the experiences continue to promote the framework's expectations. This is why the evaluation process must be continuous and the feedback must impact on design.

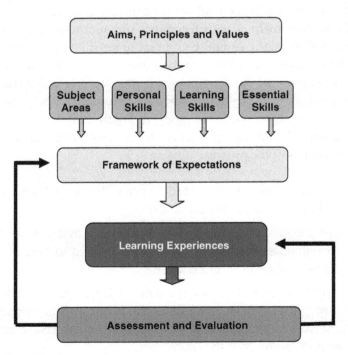

Figure 12.4 Keeping an overview

The overall model of interactive evaluation

The main purpose of evaluation is to help get the design process right. So the evaluation must interact with the design process to be effective. It must feed back into the present experience to shape its development, into the next experience to ensure it builds on what has just been learned, and into the framework itself to ensure that it is relevant to each group of students (Figure 12.4).

High-quality design is the most important part of quality assurance. If we get this right, then we can be sure that we shall be successful. This is the process of intelligent curriculum design.

Co-ordinating the processes of assessment and evaluation is one of many organizational issues that arise from different approaches to the curriculum. The more significant the curriculum change, the more significant the implications for the structure and organization. How do we get people to work differently in these ways?

That is the focus of the next section.

SECTION IV

How do we get from here to there?

13 Managing institutional dimensions

> **Restructure Again?**
> The senior leadership team is ensconced in the conference room debating on the departmental results from last year's examinations. They are concerned about variability. The evidence that 'in-school variation' in student performance is greater than 'between-school variation' is weighing heavily.
>
> Why do some departments outperform others with the same teaching groups? Should they insist on departments following the lead of the more successful ones in terms of streaming and setting of students? Well, they could, except, as a deputy points out, two of the most successful departments do things very differently and two of the worst performing do the same as the very best.
>
> Frustration is evident.
>
> 'Maybe we need to restructure', says a lone voice.

The process of curriculum design is about creating the learning experiences that our students need in order to achieve the goals that we set. We have seen that these goals are generally wide, and encompass the attainment of good GCSE passes as well as personal development and the competencies that will equip young people for the future. Determination to achieve such a curriculum may need a rethink of some present practices, and, eventually, getting some members of staff to work in different ways. This is not always as difficult as it seems, and even apparently reluctant reformers often respond much more positively than expected when given the opportunity to work in different ways, especially when students respond positively and behaviour improves. Many members of staff have just been waiting for the opportunity to work differently.

Some staff at the school in the Olympic Games scenario in Chapter 3 were sceptical about the Friday project and reluctant to 'give up' some of their lessons. But when the project got under way, they could see the value and were impressed by the way the students worked together and the manner in which they handled concepts that had seemed so difficult in lessons. In Chapter 11, we looked at a school that started to teach a GCSE maths course through BTEC engineering. This change was made because staff were given the opportunity to see how well students worked in the more practical environment of engineering, and so saw the benefits of making the change themselves. The leadership of the school did not impose the change; it created the situation in which staff wanted to change. The structure of change came from the way students needed to learn. It was not a structural change for the benefit of the organization.

In the opening scenario of this chapter, the school needed to look at the sort of learning going on in the less successful groups. Although successful departments seemed to be doing things differently, it is very likely that there was some common factor or central core of approach that was the same, even though it played out differently in different contexts. We need to understand the need for change in order to commit to it, and also to understand exactly what change is necessary. It is no good just 'restructuring again'!

There are two challenges for school leadership: first, creating the right organization structure for the curriculum and, second, ensuring staff 'buy in' to the new approaches. The importance of these two is emphasized by a range of researchers in the field such as Wenger (1998) and Fullan (2001).

The organizational structure needed will depend upon the extent to which present practices are enabling the school to attain its goals. Perhaps the goals themselves have changed. Perhaps the goals are the same, but there is a recognition that new ways need to be sought in order to attain them. Whatever the situation, the key is to identify the elements that need to change. We have looked at many in this book, but let us take three key ones to illustrate the point:

1. Introducing a clearer structure of competencies across the subjects (Chapter 7).
2. Creating space to benefit from the deeper learning than can result from the connections between subjects (Chapter 6).

3. Changing the timetable to allow time to be allocated according to learning need (Chapter 10).

How does an institution go about making these changes? Is a meeting of the senior management team held to agree on the change and then to issue a directive to staff? We all know that successful change will only come about if we get staff to sign up, and that comes when everyone can see the point and benefit. Where do we start on this?

Introducing competencies

The group of schools in Chapter 12 approached this by working with local employers to draw up the 'work skills passport' and the list was discussed with teachers, students and parents – so there was a good consensus and 'buy-in'. The passport provided a way of checking whether the skills were being developed, but did not show how they would be acquired. So the next stage was to agree on how the skills would be built into the curriculum. Meetings with heads of departments usually found the same response as the select school in Chapter 7: they all agreed that these skills should be developed, but everyone said that they had no time to teach them: 'We struggle to get through the syllabus as it is'.

Luckily the schools had already arranged for some departments (a coalition of the willing) to pilot some ideas, so there were people on hand to show how it could be done. Once they saw it was not only possible, but also beneficial, departments signed up to 'covering' at least one of the skills. Once they started, the departments found that it is actually quite difficult to cover only one skill at a time because the sorts of learning experiences that promote one skill tend to promote others as well. The change soon developed its own momentum.

Creating time for integrated learning

Most schools that have started working in this way have moved gradually. Luckily, it does not need a 'big-bang' approach. The usual first step is to plan a one-off challenge day or half-day for a particular year group where students work in teams on some sort of project that involves a number of subjects. These days can become more frequent and can be extended.

Elements of subject programmes of study are planned for these days so that they become an integral part of the curriculum and not just recreational 'fun' days – although students generally find them fun. When they see how well the approach works, schools tend to hold them weekly or extend these days into weeks. Many schools find that attendance is much better during these integrated days or weeks as students vote with their feet.

Building flexibility into the timetable

This is usually a matter of creating the possibility, and giving the permission, for teachers to co-operate in flexibility. In most fixed timetables, it would be very difficult for two teachers to say, 'Can I keep my Year 8 group all morning next week, and then you can have them the week after?' The knock-on implications around the timetable are too great, and far too many people are involved to make such decisions. So the way forward is to see the timetable, and so the school, as a series of isolated parcels, so that changes in one area are contained within that area and do not spill over into other areas. This means that three or four teachers can come to an agreement about the timetable for one week, without it affecting any other teacher. The three factors that help are reducing the number of teachers for any one class (this means that there are fewer people to negotiate with), lengthening the sessions (meaning there are fewer blocks to change) and allocating staff to one area of the school (to stop knock-on effects around the school). This is often accomplished as part of the 'schools-within-a-school' arrangement, where staff work in one section of the school only.

Schools generally find that, at first, teachers tend to stick to the timetable, but that gradually more and more changes are made. Innovation is both gradual and organic.

All of these changes are able to be made incrementally without totally abandoning previous practices. Schools can gradually move towards a different way of working, ensuring that each step is successful before the next is taken. The lone voice calling for restructuring can be ignored! But what would make such change difficult? Why have we all not done it already? There are many factors that might be in play here, and it is worth looking at them to ensure that they do not get in the way of students' learning.

The leadership structure and philosophy

Most secondary schools have subject departments as the spine of their institutional management, and so the system is embedded in the whole institution. So any suggestion about integrating subjects can be seen as a threat to the heads of department structure, and so to the leadership itself. Also, leaders are often concerned that any change to the subject system will be seen as abandoning all sense of the traditional structure of learning itself.

The budget usually dictates the extent to which the school can afford to employ heads of departments. The bigger the budget, the more likely it is that there will be more heads of departments and consequently more departments. The curriculum ends up mirroring the management structure of the school, rather than vice versa. People become reluctant to move to an integrated approach because they fear losing their place in the management structure; they worry about losing their domains.

Whether the school wants to promote itself to the public as traditional or modern also impacts on the curriculum. In a traditional school, there will be traditional subject departments. This is a public statement of philosophy along with aspects of uniform, homework and behaviour codes. If this is the image that the school wishes to project, then subject department structures fit easily.

The age and design of the school building

The basic design of schools has not changed over many years, and the classroom was conceived originally as a place where students could sit and write. As a result, sitting and writing is often the easiest thing to do in them and becomes the prevalent activity. So the design of learning is often built around the building itself. We may recognize that learning should be active, practical and open-ended with students co-operating with each other in groups to solve problems, but then find that the design of the classroom makes this difficult and so we expect them to learn in some less effective way. What is the alternative? Can we move outside of the classroom, work outdoors, go to other facilities in town or use workplaces? This has a knock-on impact on the timetable, because these sorts of arrangements require longer time slots. Innovation drives itself, but the goal is always improved learning – not change for change's sake.

Schools do have specialized facilities, such as laboratories, workshops, studios, playing fields and gymnasia. The tendency is to allocate these specialist facilities to the appropriate departments. But that assumes that all the learning in these departments demands the specialist facilities, and none of the learning in the other departments requires them. Is all learning in science practical and dependent on a laboratory? Is no learning in maths ever practical? Might not other subjects be better taught in a laboratory from time to time? A key question for leadership is the extent to which students need to spend time in specialist rooms on a weekly, monthly or annual basis, and the value in students having laboratory time if, when for some aspects of learning, they do not need these facilities.

The pressure to change

A school with a strong examination record has relatively little pressure to change. A school with a weak examination record is likely to be expected to change. However, the change expected is seldom one of innovation, or tackling the root causes of the poor record. But this does not need to be so in either case. In Chapter 7, we looked at the school with 100 per cent A*–C passes that, nevertheless, undertook a change in its curriculum to build in competencies. The schools in the scenarios involved in putting maths into BTEC engineering, basic work around the Humber Bridge, and forensic science were all schools with poor GCSE records that improved examination passes significantly by moving away from traditional approaches.

Is one type of organization better than the rest?

To make this judgement, we have to go back to our aims. If we are trying to develop young people as independent learners, critical thinkers, teamworkers and problem solvers, then there are clearly implications for the type of organization and institution that will be most successful. A rigid system that enforces strict discipline and emphasizes the authority of teachers and the need to work individually without talking is unlikely to bring about these sorts of aims. When we spoke about attitudes, values and dispositions in Chapter 2, we suggested that these would be developed through the ethos of the school, the approaches to learning that it takes and the pattern of relationships that prevail.

The learning outcomes for young people are not achieved through the internal organization of the institution, but through the quality of the curriculum design and the extent to which it is well taught. There are, though, important areas of institutional organization to consider.

Setting, streaming and mixed ability

The basic premise is that learning is linear and incremental, and therefore some students will make swifter progress than others. The wider the range of success or the longer the line of students who pass each learning checkpoint, the greater is the challenge for the teacher in presenting the next stages of learning. Questions of setting, streaming and mixed ability are organizational issues built on principles about the best way to deal with different levels of ability and prior achievement.

But this does not take account of the nature of the learning experiences that can be provided. Where these experiences are rich, and where students are engaged in open-ended activities where they have some independence to follow their own lines of enquiry, then it is possible for all the students to be learning at their own level within the same activity. However, where learning experiences are narrow and didactic, and where students are all learning exactly the same thing at the same time at the direction of the teacher, then they cannot all learn at their own level.

The implications are clear. If learning experiences are narrow and didactic, then we shall need some form of setting or streaming. If learning experiences are rich and enabling, then we can have mixed ability groups. The big mistake is to move to mixed ability groups but retain narrow and didactic teaching.

Of course, the reason for designing rich and open-ended learning experiences is not just to cope with mixed ability groups, but because most things are learned better this way. So if most learning is best done this way, then there is seldom any need for setting and streaming.

The need is seldom, but, of course, there are times when some students will need a particular form of support. In the previous chapter, we looked at Amrit who was sometimes in a group of 150 students watching a demonstration (the whole year group, so inevitably mixed ability) and at other times in a group of five for coaching in maths. The coaching group was a temporary 'set' selected because these students all needed the same sort of help with a particular topic. The next coaching session might be with a different group.

An alternative or supplementary curriculum

For some students, the traditional secondary school curriculum fails to engage. From a combination of experiences outside or inside school, they have learned over the years that they are unlikely to succeed so there is little value to them in the whole process. As a result, they might behave badly, fail to turn up, rebel, cause trouble or simply accept that school life is a drag and let inertia take over. Most schools do everything they can to help these students, and have staff dedicated to their support and progress; but for a small proportion of young people school holds little prospect for the future and serves instead as a demonstration of how they are destined to be life's less successful people.

But this success is usually measured by schools, and by these unsuccessful students themselves, in terms of the 'leaves' in our 'tree' model. This is where they have been tested, judged and found wanting. But we seldom consider the roots of learning in these situations. In Chapter 3, we noticed that some students start school at the age of 11 (and even start primary school at 5) with a well developed set of roots. This makes learning easy for them and so they succeed. But what about the roots of those students who find learning difficult and who eventually give up and rebel? Could it be that they find learning difficult because they have poorly developed roots? Because they have not developed the key competencies of investigation, critical thinking, working independently, problem solving and because they lack the basic

3Cs, they cannot succeed in terms of the leaves. We have often tried to remedy this by spending even more time on the leaves, when we might have had more success had we spend more time helping them develop the roots.

We often characterize the less successful students as having 'low ability' or 'less aptitude' or even a 'low IQ'. The last is particularly interesting, because almost all recent research indicates that whatever IQ is, it does not seem to be static. There are numerous examples of people who are written off at school, but who succeed in later life. The English Open University is based on this very notion that failure to succeed at school does not mean someone is not capable of gaining a degree later on. But what happens to these people? Did their IQ suddenly improve? Or did subsequent experiences enable their roots to develop?

International studies such as the Organisation for Economic Co-operation and Development's (OECD) Performance Indicators of Student Attainment (PISA) indicate that right across the world, students from deprived backgrounds tend to have poorer educational performance than those from more wealthy backgrounds. It is a tendency rather than an immutable rule, and there are many exceptions. But there is no international consensus as to why this should be the case. Perhaps it is because international researchers have been looking at the leaves instead of looking at the roots. Those schools in deprived areas that buck the trend tend to have strong programmes for developing learning skills, and for building self-confidence.

Some students are trying to grow their roots on very stony ground and have every blight imaginable attacking their tree. So it is all the more important to help those roots develop. Stony ground need not prevent fruitful growth – just look at a vineyard.

Most schools do all they can to avoid exclusion and often use an alternative curriculum'. Usually, the school 'outsources' the learning diet for a student or a small group of students to a provider who tries to meet their needs within the security of a separate environment. The provider undertakes to provide a bespoke curriculum offer, and the student undertakes to attempt to fulfil the expectations. Usually, these experiences are highly practical, and emphasize the social and emotional aspects of development. There is often an attempt to encourage the student to take a vocational course and gain a qualification at an entry levels. In fact, they focus on the roots. For such students, the curriculum they meet and the people who provide it can be a lifeline.

Of course, you might wonder why this sort of curriculum is only provided after the incidents that might have led to exclusion. Might it not have been better to provide a suitable curriculum in the first place? The alternative curriculum should be on the menu from the start, not only when all else fails.

Curriculum transition from primary to secondary school

The vast majority of students look forward to their new school (and to the fulfilment of the promises made when schools sought to attract parental preference!) They are looking forward to the newness, so successful transition does not necessarily mean replicating the primary school in Year 7. Students enjoy meeting the specialist subjects for the first time, and their first impressions can be lasting, so what would we want to convey about a subject? The fun of the subject? Or the fascination of the big ideas and the big questions associated with the subject? Or is it the rules and the required working routines?

If students meet the big ideas early on in ways that are accessible to them, they are likely to develop further the inbuilt fascination that they bring with them to their new school. Induction into the new department can mean induction into the excitement of new ideas and the fascination of a new discipline. New students need to feel that are good at the subject, and be given belief in their success for the rest of their year might.

Many schools are now looking again at Year 7 and the experiences that the students will face. These schools sometimes have a cross-curricular team of teachers who are assigned to consolidate the learning experience of the students for all or part of their weekly timetable. Usually, the school runs parallel provision where the subject departments offer some focused lessons and the cross-curricular team offers a series of sessions, often extended to a day or more, incorporating a range of the other subjects.

Some schools offer a 'Learning for Life' curriculum in Year 7, where the basic skill areas of literacy and numeracy form the bedrock. Others offer a 'Creative Curriculum' where the humanities or arts provide the impetus. Many see a themed approach as vital as this shows coherence in learning for students. They would also argue that students will also benefit from a smoother transition from their primary experience.

Homework

What matters is not how much homework there should be, but how good it is. A lot of poor homework simply serves to put the learner off learning. A little excellent homework may well have the opposite effect. In recent years, schools have begun to look more closely at homework as curriculum provision, rather than as a form of discipline. As we said in Chapter 1, learning takes place across the entire planned learning experience: in lessons, events, routines and what students do before and after school hours. Homework is part of the beyond school hours provision and well used it is an important element of curriculum design.

Using student voice to influence learning and teaching

One of the aspects of infrastructure that can make a difference to curriculum impact is taking account of the views of students. Over recent years, schools have set up systems to garner the views of students, usually in some sort of school council arrangement. From these views, schools have been able to ensure that learning fits students needs and engages their commitment.

Real world problems motivate learners. Their own learning is something in which the majority of learners are interested and want to influence. The school needs the confidence to practise what it writes in its aims: the bits about 'reaching full potential', 'active engagement' and 'growing responsibility'. Schools that have given real responsibility to learners report changes in culture, relationships and motivation in students. They also report improved outcomes: more responsible citizens, more confident individuals and more successful learners.

One local education authority in England commissioned a survey of students' views of their school. The survey asked questions such as, 'Do you feel supported at school?', 'Do your teachers explain things clearly?' and 'Is your learning interesting'. They collated the information and when the local inspectors visited schools, instead of discussing why the school was in the bottom quartile for GCSE passes, they discussed why it was in the bottom quartile for students feeling supported. When schools started focusing on these issues, they found that their GCSE passes improved anyway. Student voice is not an optional extra – it is a key driver of improvement.

Surveying students' views on learning

Some schools have started to use surveys to help bring better learning to the learner. POST (Pupil Online Survey Tool) is used by secondary schools in the Black Country area of England (in the industrial West Midlands) to offer students the chance to give their views online about the criteria for effective lessons. Basically, the students identify, with help, ten criteria which are amended and approved by the senior leadership team in the school. The list in Figure 13.1 is typical.

Students then complete an online survey and the analysis shows how effective each department is on each criteria. The example in Figure 13.2 shows the results in terms of the D&T department. You can see where D&T features and which are the top two departments in the school for each criterion. Each department sees only its own score and the top two; not the rest. The survey is repeated over the next three half terms.

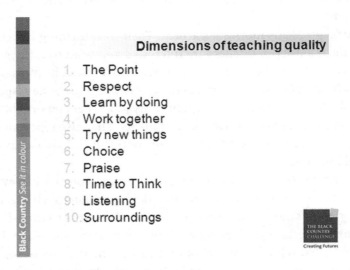

Figure 13.1 Dimensions of quality
Source: *Pupil On-line Survey,* Black Country Challenge (2010).

	2 Getting Help – Do you receive support whem stuck on problem in class?
	Answered 'Always' or 'Regularly'
Design Technology	66.3%
Modern Foreign Languages	65.1%
	64.0%
	62.3%
	60.6%
	59.4%
	58.9%
	56.6%
	53.1%
	52.0%
	49.7%
	43.4%
	39.4%

	3 Choice – How often are you offered a choice of what to do during lessons?
	Answered 'Always' or 'Regularly'
PE	28.7%
Music	24.7%
	17.2%
	16.1%
Design Technology	14.9%
	13.8%
	13.2%
	12.1%
	11.5%
	9.8%
	7.5%
	7.5%
	6.9%

	6 Group Work – How often do you work in a pair or a small group on a shared activity?
	Answered 'Always' or 'Regularly'
PE	75.9%
Music	61.5%
	46.0%
	44.3%
	40.8%
	29.9%
	29.3%
Design Technology	24.7%
	19.0%
	17.2%
	16.7%
	12.6%

	7 Being Creative and Active – How often are you creative or active in your lessons? e.g. making things, role play, practical work.
	Answered 'Always' or 'Regularly'
	68.8%
	60.1%
	59.5%
	45.1%
	35.8%
	32.4%
	27.7%
	27.2%
	27.2%
	23.7%
	18.5%
	12.1%
	11.6%

Figure 13.2 Student voice
Source: *Pupil On-line Survey,* Black Country Challenge (2010).

What happens is that the departments towards the bottom of any list ask those at the top what they do, how they do it and whether they can watch their lessons. What also happens is that the gap between top and bottom shrinks and students get a more consistent experience across departments. There will always be a table from top to bottom, but the gap between top and bottom reduces. The two tables in Figure 13.3 show some fascinating trends in terms of students' views.

Within the two terms the students have graded the bottom department as being 21 per cent better than at the time of the first survey and much nearer the best than previously.

This is an example of the student voice having a real effect because the staff want to do what they are trying to do: make learning as effective as possible. They just need to enlist the help of the people that want to be helped.

The senior team who at the start of this chapter were discussing the variation in performance between departments had a significant challenge. Rather than consider restructuring, the challenge might be to test out the

	OVERALL (1)			OVERALL (3)	
RANK	SUBJECT	%AGREE	RANK	SUBJECT	%AGREE
1	Drama	85%	1	Design & tech	89%
2	Art & Design	81%	2	Geography	88%
3	*****	75%	3	*****	86%
4	*****	74%	4	*****	84%
5	*****	73%	5	*****	82%
6	*****	72%	5	*****	82%
7	ORIGAMI	70%	5	ORIGAMI	82%
7	*****	70%	6	*****	80%
8	*****	65%	7	*****	79%
8	*****	65%	8	*****	76%
9	*****	59%	9	*****	71%
10	*****	57%	10	*****	70%
11	*****	33%	11	*****	68%

Figure 13.3 Student responses
Source: *Pupil On-line Survey,* Black Country Challenge (2010).

effectiveness of the way that learning meets students' needs. Schools that have systems for using student voice well have a natural impetus for improving curriculum design.

This section on making it all work ends where the book started: with a focus on how to make sure there is impact on students' progress. Every school sets out with that intent. The ways in which this can be accomplished are numerous. There is not just one recipe for success. If there were, we would all have found it by now and would be using it.

But there is a very wide variety of options available to us. We can select from this variety and adapt it to meet our own needs. We are not as constrained by a national curriculum and national regulations as we think and have more flexibility than we realize. Many schools have found surprisingly radical approaches that have brought them success. We do not all have to be so radical, but the examples do show us the variety of options available. This is the subject of the next chapter.

14 A variety of options

The Week-long Lesson
The dance troupe is sitting on the studio floor, exhausted but elated, after a whole week of rehearsals that has ended successfully in a performance for a video. A week of strenuous physical activity, but also of artistic creativity: developing the choreography, perfecting the movements, ensuring that costume and set complement the artistic purpose. They have worked through each day and late into the evening, but it has all been worthwhile, and they now sit sharing the sense of exhausted satisfaction of artistic achievement.

These are Year 10 students who have just completed an important coursework element of their PE GCSE.

The practice of the school day being made up of a number of subject-focused lessons is so ingrained in the profession that it is hard to envisage anything else. Yet here is a school whose GCSE programme comes in week-long sessions. Now you might have thought that of all the subjects, the one that you couldn't do for a whole week would be PE – you'd get too tired. But here are these Year 10s, tired but immensely proud of their achievement.

Working from the goals

The various scenarios that we have looked at through this book have illustrated a wide variety of approaches to curriculum design. Some have been quite radical; some were radical once but have now become mainstream. There is an almost endless variety of options. What they have in common is that they have been adopted for a purpose; not just to do something new.

In each case, the school has started with the question, 'What are we trying to achieve?' and moved from there to 'How shall we organize learning?' The particular form of organization has been adopted in order to achieve a particular goal. The reason for the 'week-long lesson' was that the school's goals were to develop competencies in investigation, problem solving, co-operation, independence and critical thinking. These goals require students to be involved in more open-ended learning experiences where they can investigate, work in teams and solve problems. This cannot be accomplished in a 40-minute lesson, or even in a one or two-hour lesson. So over a period of time, the school extended the length of 'lessons' to the point where much of the GCSE programme is followed in week-long units. As well as removing the time usually wasted in moving from lesson to lesson, a week gives students time to get into an investigation in depth. It also concentrates students' mind on the task in hand; instead of having two years to get their coursework done, they have to complete it in the week. This was one of several unintended or unforeseen consequences.

Another key consequence, not entirely unforeseen, was that it changed the nature of the teaching and learning transaction. On the whole, the traditional teaching style has been evolved around the short(ish) subject focus lesson. As you extend the length of the lesson, teachers tend to extend their teaching style over the longer period. This has the effect of negating the advantage of the longer period and is often the reason why schools suggest that longer periods will not work. However, the school found that there was a 'tipping point' where the lesson became so long that the traditional teaching approaches could no longer be used. When you have the whole week, the teacher can no longer be the person at the front directing learning the whole time. This means that more open-ended learning experiences need to be designed that have their own momentum and which students themselves can develop: experiences in which students have to co-operate with others to investigate things and solve problems. Faced with a whole week with the same class, teachers begin to think, 'We can't spend all week in the same room, we'll have to get out and visit somewhere', and, of course, there is the time and flexibility to do so. Teachers also think, 'It can't just be me all week, I'll need to arrange some visitors or colleagues to input'. The very nature of learning begins to change.

Another thing that changes is the relationship between teacher and student. The school reported that half-way through the first morning the disruptive pupils (and they had many) began to tire of being disruptive. Importantly, that middle group of pupils who can get drawn into disruption became fed up with the disrupters. It seems that they can go to another lesson and start the disruption process over again, but find it hard to sustain the process over a longer time. Perhaps, like the traditional teacher, their techniques were evolved for a different system.

The changed relationship is also to do with the different model of learning. Where students are more independently engaged in a longer-term project, the teaching role becomes more of consultant and adviser. Instead of having to make students work, teachers found that they were taking more of a back seat as the work progressed, and relationships improved.

This resulted in less stress for the teachers, and for the students. It also, interestingly, meant less time preparing lessons. When students are set open-ended investigative tasks in which they work with some independence, there is no need for a whole series of lesson plans. Once the open-ended task has been set up the teacher cannot be sure where the learning will go, so cannot be writing plans for each day. It means being quicker on your feet to shape learning as it occurs, but less writing of plans. Teachers find this much more congenial, and some say that working in this way was the reason they came into the profession in the first place.

Set out like this, the approach sounds like a universal panacea. It is certainly not easy to start this off (it is no good going into school tomorrow and telling some unfortunate member of staff that they have 9D for geography all next week) and needs a great deal of thought and preparation. It is best to move in easy stages, although there will always be the necessity for the 'tipping point' where things suddenly become clearer and easier.

It is not being suggested that everything can be learned best in week-long chunks. Some things are best learned in short bursts, some need constant practice and repetition. Even within the same subject, there will be units that will be best learned in extended periods, and others that will need shorter periods. This is the flexible timetable that we discussed in Chapter 10.

However, the week-long lesson does help illustrate the variety of options. What is important is that any new approach is adopted because it will help attain one or more of our goals. We are not talking about innovation for its own sake, but we are talking about a willingness to rethink aspects of practice that may be longstanding, but that do not contribute to the goals.

The 48-week year

Faced with poor attendance, and students struggling to gain GCSE passes because they had missed so much time, some schools have managed to extend the school year. Some are open almost all year round. Before you blanch at the thought of losing your holidays, read on. The law requires students to attend school for 190 days a year, but it does not say that they all have to attend on the same 190 days. If your school is open most of the year, missed days can be made up at some later time. This changes the dynamic significantly. When the school is open only for the 190 days, a student can be punished for missing a day, but the day can never be made up. This way it can. It is also the answer to parents who, quite sensibly, want to take a holiday during normal term time when everything is cheaper. No problem to be away for two weeks in June, you can make it up in August. This actually suits many parents well.

Of course, the teachers don't have to work all year; they have to do their 190 days. They sign up for their holidays just as you would in an office. You can't have everyone off at once. They can even be paid overtime for teaching extra days. The great advantage is that they too can take holidays in term time when it's cheaper.

You may have spotted the issue. It was raised by heads of departments when the system was suggested. They all complained that if students missed a week of their course then they would certainly not pass their GCSE. The issue was, of course, that with such poor attendance, many students were already missing far more than a week. That was one of the reasons why they were doing so badly. So the courses were run over a set period that was similar to the normal year with revision classes and catch-up sessions added on. Students missing time during the year caught up later on. Many students with good attendance stayed on anyway for extra lessons and revision.

The system also cut truancy. Knowing that days had to be made up later seemed to make students more reluctant to stay away.

The ten-hour day

In response to poor attendance and lateness from many students who were also carers, or were in difficult home circumstances, some schools have extended the school day. Students, and teachers, opt for an early or late shift. Linked to a course system, students can pick their way through their programmes keeping to times that suit their home circumstances or biological clocks. Many teachers prefer to come in early and finish at lunchtime. Many others prefer to spend the morning in bed. You can have a choice!

Stage or age?

Schools across the world tend to arrange their pupils into age-based classes. Like the Roman Cohorts, having been recruited together they stay in that year group for evermore. Outside of school, learning tends to be different. If you enrol in a night-school class to learn French, they do not ask you how old you are, but how good you are at French. Should you be in the beginners group, the intermediate or the advanced? They certainly don't want to know whether you were born in August or September.

Most schools go some way along this road with students put into sets according to their prior attainment, but these sets are usually within a year group anyway. Some schools have shown that it is possible to go beyond this and run the whole school along night-school lines, or along the lines of North American universities with a credit-based system for courses.

In these approaches, the Key Stage 3 subject programmes have been designed as credit courses at three different levels. To complete Key Stage 3 (the first three years of secondary education in England) in a subject a number of credit courses must be taken at each level, and, like universities, there are choices and you generally have to do Level 1 courses before Level 2. Some courses count towards more than one subject, or have a vocational dimension. Through this element of choice and students taking more of fewer courses at one level before moving on, students soon became mixed up in terms of year groups. Some could complete Key Stage 3 early and start on a similar programme through GCSE courses, or take longer on Key Stage 3. The school made an arrangement with the local College of Further Education to have the courses recognized towards their own awards so that the students could move on.

Such a system takes a lot of work to set up, and may not be necessary in many schools. In this school the goal was to provide flexible pathways for students who did not do well within the traditional approach and needed a more personalized approach. This way, some could take longer, while others moved quickly to GCSE. If you do not have that goal, you would not want this approach. It is mentioned to indicate the variety of options.

The flexible timetable

If you visit schools, you are often taken to see the timetable. Once these were on paper, then Lego blocks, and now they are shown on screen. These are monuments to human ingenuity and the ability to manipulate multiple variables for the benefit of all concerned. In one school the head indicated this complex pattern of times, students, teachers, rooms and subjects and said, 'The last time I checked, teachers were ignoring this for almost 50 per cent of the time. I shall be happy when it's 100 per cent of the time'.

How do they do this? And how come the head is so happy? (And what does the timetabler think?)

And, of course, why are they doing this?

The goal in this case was to give the opportunity for more open-ended and extended learning, but retain the flexibility for some learning to be in shorter chunks. One way of doing this is for all teachers or departments to send their requests in to the timetabler as we discussed in Chapter 10. The poor timetabler then has to make a timetable that is even more complex than usual. The other way is to devolve the timetable to teachers.

The key to making this work was to reduce the number of teachers any class saw in a week, and the number of lessons there were in a day. That way, a small number of teachers can talk among themselves and make decisions about how to organize the week.

The school effected this through three changes. The day was divided into three 2-hour periods (Fridays were shorter). This required only three teachers in a day. Subjects were divided into six faculties, and it was agreed that a teacher should be able to teach any subject in their faculty at Key Stage 3 (there was a thematic approach anyway). This meant that students have only six teachers in a week. A further refinement was a 'schools-within-a-school' approach so that the same teachers were allocated to a restricted set of classes rather than spread across the school. This meant that the timetable had 'firewalls', and changes in one area did not automatically impact on all other areas.

These three changes meant that on any given day, three teachers could agree to shorten or lengthen sessions because the changes did not affect anyone else. Six could change the pattern for the whole week or year. They were doing so almost 50 per cent of the time. And the head hoped it would be 100 per cent, because it meant that time was being allocated according to immediate learning need on a dynamic basis by the people best placed to make the decision.

History has not recorded what the timetabler thought of this.

Making the most of the options

Selecting the right option for our goals can allow us to maximize learning. By choosing the option that best meets your goals, you can design a curriculum that can give students deeper knowledge and understanding within the subject area. Such a curriculum can equip them with the skills they need to live their lives successfully in the twenty-first century. It can make them lifelong learners.

In doing so, it will give them all they need to enter adulthood with the confidence, the ability and the desire to make the world a better place.

If we achieve that, then we shall truly have a world-class curriculum.

15 Postscript – A world-class curriculum

> **A Flood of Ideas**
>
> A school in India is set alongside one of the upper tributaries of the Ganges. This river had seldom flooded until recently, but climate change is melting the glaciers and floods are becoming common. The school made this a topic of study. The children consulted village elders to gain their wisdom about how they coped with previous floods. They took measurements and constructed high platforms where school equipment could be stored above flood level. They made lifejackets out of plastic water bottles, and took courses on resuscitation. They lobbied the local government about flood defences, and started a website to bring public attention to their plight. Their work involved maths, science, geography, technology, communication, citizenship and a whole range of leaves. It was rooted in their own experience and their own locality, it had a strong real and moral purpose and the children had a compelling emotional commitment.
>
> Their story is now on the website of the British Council (www. britishcouncil.org/savinglives). These are truly global citizens.

The introduction to this book referred to the notion of a World-Class Curriculum, and suggested that there might be a set of principles and approaches that would take a curriculum way beyond the ordinary and sufficient, and make it truly 'world class'. These principles and approaches would apply in any country whatever the national curriculum. They take learning beyond the national and approach the universal. This is the way to create a curriculum for global citizens.

These world-class principles would be about the way the country's national curriculum is turned into learning experiences for children that are exciting and uplifting, that recognize the individuality of every child, and which encourage their development as human beings.

If we were to pull together the strands that run through this book, certain principles stand out, as can be observed in Figure PS.1.

Principles of a World-Class Curriculum

A world-class curriculum will:

- inspire and challenge all learners, and equip them with the confidence, the ability and desire to make the world a better place
- be based on clear, shared aims, principles and values that put the learner at their heart
- excite imaginations and give learners access to the world's major areas of learning
- promote personal development and the key competencies of learning and life
- be located in the context of the learner's life, and emphasise the interconnectedness of learning
- provide for intellectual, physical, emotional, social, scientific, aesthetic and creative development
- be international in its outlook, but rooted within its community
- address contemporary issues as well as the big ideas that have shaped the world in the past
- promote independence of thought and creativity of mind through a wide range of learning approaches

Figure PS.1 Principles of a world-class curriculum

These are a set of aspirations that will guide the development of curriculum change within a school. They could also become the touchstone or benchmark by which a curriculum is evaluated, and by which schools could work together in partnership to create and endorse such a curriculum.

The Curriculum Foundation (a not-for-profit organization) is developing the notion of professional peer evaluation against such principles as a way of promoting a world-class curriculum. You can find out more at www. curriculumfoundation.org. The process of curriculum design should be a corporate one, a matter of professional co-operation. Working with other schools is not only professionally rewarding, it is the best way of extending our own ideas, developing the creativity of our approach, and designing the very best curriculum we can set before the children, wherever they are in the world.

At the beginning of this book, we set out the ambition that the curriculum should equip every young person to enter adulthood with the confidence, the ability and the desire to make the world a better place. We can achieve that ambition if we ourselves are ambitious about what the curriculum can achieve. Through our design, we can unleash the full power of the curriculum and make learning irresistible.

Glossary

'A' Level	Advanced Level – a public examination usually taken at age 18
Attainment target	the learning expectations for each of the subjects in the English National Curriculum in terms of attainment
BTEC	one of a range of qualifications offered by the Business and Technology Education Council
CBI	Confederation of British Industry
Competency	a combination of knowledge, skill and attitude within an area of operation
D&T	design and technology
3Cs	basic competencies in Communication, Calculation and use of Computers
Curriculum dimensions	seven themes running across the English secondary curriculum
EYFS	Early Years Foundation Stage: the stage of education before compulsory schooling
Functional skills	elements of English, maths and ICT that contribute to basic competence in these areas
GCSE	General Certificate of Secondary Education
ICT	Information and Communication Technology

Key stage	The English National Curriculum is divided into four key stages: Key Stage 1: Years 1 and 2 (ages 5–7) Key Stage 2: Years 3–6 (ages 7–11) Key Stage 3: Years 7–9 (ages 11–14) Key Stage 4: Years 10 and 11 (ages 14–16)
Level description	specification of attainment at eight levels within an attainment target
Local authority	an elected body responsible for education within an English county
NEET	Not in Education, Employment or Training
NVQ	National Vocational Qualification
Ofsted	Office for Standards in Education, Children's Services and Skills
PE	physical education
PLTS	Personal, Learning and Thinking Skills
Programme of study	the knowledge, skills and understanding that need to be taught in each subject at each key stage
QCA	The former Qualifications and Curriculum Authority that oversaw the national curriculum in England. It later became the Qualifications and Curriculum Development Agency (QCDA) before being closed in 2011
RE	religious education
SSAT	Specialist Schools and Academies Trust
Vocational education	education for a specific area of employment
Vocationally related	education for employment generally, as distinct from a specific area of employment
Year group	grouping of students within a school. The school year in England runs from September to August, and children born between these dates constitute a year group.

References

Ananiadou, K. & Claro, M. (2009) '21st century skills and competences for new millennium learners in OECD countries.' OECD Education Working Paper, No. 41. DOI: 10.1787/218525261154.

Anderson, L. W. & Krathwohl, D. R. (eds) (2001) *A Taxonomy for Learning, Teaching, and Assessing: A Revision of Bloom's Taxonomy of Educational Objectives*. New York: Longman.

Barnes, D. & Todd, F. (1995) *Communication and Learning Revisited: Making Meaning through Talk*. Portsmouth, NH: Boynton/Cook.

Becta (2008) *Emerging Technologies for Learning*, 3, March 2008. Coventry: Becta.

Bennett, S. N. (1976) *Teaching Styles and Pupil Progress*. London: Open Books.

Blatchford, P., Hallam, J., Ireson, J., Kutnik, P. with Creech, A. (2008) 'Classes, groups and transitions: Structures for teaching and learning.' *Primary Review Research Briefings*, 9/2. Cambridge: Cambridge University Press.

Bloom, B. (ed.) (1956) *The Taxonomy of Educational Objectives: The Classification of Educational Goals, Handbook I: Cognitive Domain*. New York: Susan Fauer.

Bruner, J. S. (1966) *Towards a Theory of Instruction*. Cambridge, MA: Harvard University Press.

Craft, A. (2008). *Voyages of Discovery: Looking at Models of Engagement*. London: Creative Partnerships London North.

De Groot, A. (1965) *Thought and Choice in Chess*. Mouton The Hague (in Hirsch, E. D., 1987).

Desforges, C., Fox, R., Muir, D. & Slater, A. (2001) *Teaching and Learning*. Oxford: Blackwell.

Dýrfjörð, K. (2006) 'The pedagogy of Reggio Emilia: Developmentally appropriate practice through the looking glass of Dewey's democracy', in Ross, A. (ed.), *Citizenship Education: Europe and the World*. London: CiCe, pp. 291–302.

Facer, K., Furlong, R. & Sutherland, R. (2003) *Screenplay: Children and Computing in the Home*. London: Routledge.

Fullan, M. (2001) *Leading in a Culture of Change*. New York: Corwin Ross.

Gardner, H. (1999) *The Disciplined Mind*. London: Penguin Books.

Goswami, U. (2008) *Cognitive Development: The Learning Brain*. Cambridge: Psychology Press, Taylor & Francis.

Goswami, U. & Bryant, P. (2007) 'Children's cognitive development and learning.' *Primary Review Research Briefings*, 2/1a. Cambridge: Cambridge University Press.

Hargreaves, D. (2006) *A New Shape for Learning*. London: SSAT.

Heppell, S., Chapman, C., Millward, R., Constable, M. & Furness, J. (2004) *Building Learning Futures*. London: CABE/RIBA.

Hirsch, E. (2007) *Cultural Literacy*. New York: Houghton.

HMI (1976) *Primary Schools in England*. London: HMSO.

—(1985) *The Curriculum from 5 to 16*. London: HMSO.

Howe, C. & Mercer, N. (2007) 'Children's social development: Peer interaction and classroom learning.' *Primary Review Research Briefings*, 2/1b. Cambridge: Cambridge University Press.

Katzir, T. & Pare-Blagoev, J. (2006) 'Applying cognitive neuroscience research to education: The case of literacy.' *Educational Psychologist*, 41(1), 53–74.

Laevers, F. (2000) 'Forward to basics! Deep-level learning and the experiential approach.' *Early Years*, 20(2), 20–9.

Lave, J. & Wenger, E. (1991) *Situated Learning. Legitimate Peripheral Participation*. Cambridge: Cambridge University Press.

Marton, F. & Saljo, R. (2008) *Deep and Surface Approaches to Learning*. Sweden: University of Gottenburg.

Mercer, N. (2000) *Words and Minds: How We Use Language to Think Together*. London: Routledge.

Ofqual (2010) *Annual Report for 2010*. London: Ofqual.

Ofsted (2008a) *Learning Outside the Classroom* (ref: 0702190). London: Ofsted.

—(2008b) *Curriculum in Innovative Schools* (ref: 070097). London: Ofsted.

—(2009) *Twelve Outstanding Secondary Schools* (ref: 070170). London: Ofsted.

Pahl, K. (2005) 'Narrative spaces and multiple identities', in Marsh, J. (ed.) *Popular Culture, New Media and Digital Literacy in Early Childhood.* Abingdon: RoutledgeFalmer.

Peters, R. S. (1971) *The Logic of Education.* London: Routledge & Kegan Paul.

Phenix, P. (1986) *Realms of Meaning.* Los Angeles, CA: Printingcraft, Incorporated.

Piaget, J. (1950) *The Psychology of Intelligence.* Oxford, UK: Oxford University Press.

Qualifications and Curriculum Authority (2007a) *Annual Report.* London: QCA.

— (2007b) *The National Curriculum: Statutory Requirements for Key Stages 3 and 4.* London: QCA.

Rychen, D. S. & Tiana, A. (2004) *Developing Key Competencies in Education: Some Lessons from International and National Experience.* Geneva: UNESCO-IBE, Studies in Comparative Education.

Trapscott, D. (1998) *Grown up Digital.* New York: McGraw Hill.

Vygotsky, L. S. (1978) *Mind in Society: The Development of Higher Psychological Processes.* Cambridge, MA: Harvard University Press.

Wenger, E. (1998). *Communities of Practice: Learning, Meaning and Identity.* Cambridge, MA: Cambridge University Press.

Wolf, A. (2011) *Review of Vocational Education* (The Wolf Report). London: DFE.

Wolfe, P. (2010) *Brain Matters.* Alexandria: VA ASCD Books.

Index

age-based classes arrangement 195–6
alternative/supplementary curriculum 184–6
Anderson, Lorin 68, 75
animated film (example) 66
Apple 17
assessment 157–73
  approaches 168
  cross-department 170
  and design 159–60
  evaluation process 170–1
  formative assessment 160–1
  implications for curriculum design 169
  importance of 158–9
  interactive evaluation 173
  keeping the overview 172
  skills, complexity of 166–8
  skills, contexts for 168
  structure of 169
  within a subject 162–4

Baccalaureate (E-Bacc) 142
basic skills 35–6, 165
beach (example) 51–2
Bloom's taxonomy 67–9, 75, 78, 164
Bristol's floating harbour 120

calculation 37
church times (example) 123–4
co-construction of learning 69–70
communication 37
community 123–5
competencies 13, 35, 42, 96–105, 131, 165
  application in school 103–4
  introduction of 179
  models 98–9
  progress in 100–2
computer technology 30
  competency 37
  and vocational training 146
concepts 12
concepts links 88
Confederation of British Industry (CBI) 23, 147
content links 87
crime scene (example) 106
cross-cultural themes 83

curriculum design 7–20
  aims of 16, 191–3
  and curriculum planning, difference
    between 18
  design triangle 62–5
  and key skills 11–12
  and knowledge 12–13
  and lessons 14–15
  matrix 61–2
  and national curriculum 9–10
  and personal and social development 11
  and planning 9
  process 65
  and subjects and study programmes 10–11
  three-circle (Why, How, What) approach 17–18
Curriculum Foundation 199
curriculum frameworks 39–47
  adaptability 47
  impact in classroom 44–6
curriculum transition 186
curriculum tree 8–9, 51–65
  and curriculum design 59–61
  learning leaves 80–95
  learning roots 55–6, 66–79
  learning trunk 57–8

deeper understanding 86–8
  concepts links 88
  content links 87
  skills links 87
deep learning 66–79, 164
  in action 71
  Bloom's taxonomy 67–9
  Hargreaves model 70–1
  and key concepts 75–6
  and knowledge 71–3, 74–5
  Marton and Saljo model 69–70
  and skills 73–4
  subject skills 76–9
Desforges, Charles 169
Dickens, Charles 72–3

Early Years Foundation Stage (EYFS) guidance 11
engineering better mathematics (example) 139
England

curriculum framework 41–2
secondary skills 28
English National Curriculum 16, 24, 28–30, 57–8, 86, 118
cross-cultural themes 83–4
functional skills 28–9
level descriptions 162–3
OCR key skills 30
English Secondary Curriculum 10, 11
essentialness 29, *92*
events 14
expectations framework 165–6, 169
ex students' achievements 152–3

Finland
cross-cultural themes 83
curriculum design 26
curriculum model 43
subjects and learning 82
floods (example) 198
Four Cs 27
France 84
functional skills 28–9, 35
Further Education model 133

gateways *see* pathways and gateways
General Certificate of Secondary Education (GCSE) 16, 18
timetable 132
generic skills *see* key skills
'Go for it' scheme 150

Hadron Collider 167
Hargreaves, David 70, 75
Hawes, Trevor 109
Head Teachers and Industry 150
Hirsch, E. 81, 89, 100–2, 103, 167
homework 187
Humber Bridge (example) 117

Industrial Age model 148
'Inspire' scheme 150
institutional management 177–90
age and design of school building 181–2
alternative/supplementary curriculum 184–6
comparability 182–3
competencies introduction 179
curriculum transition 186
homework 187
integrated learning 179–80
leadership structure and philosophy 181
and pressure to change 182
setting, streaming and mixed ability 183–4
and student voice 187–8
student voice surveys 188–90

timetable flexibility 180
integrated approach 88–9, 99
irresistible learning 106–16
and adolescence 111–13
and appropriate curriculum 110–11
and authentic learning 113–15
factors 108–9
first-hand practical experiences 115
irresistible design 116
and students' imagination 110
and students' own lives 113
traditional methods 109–10

Jobs, Steve 17

key concepts 75–6
key skills 11–12, 33, *34*
King, Martin Luther 17
knowledge 12–13
importance of 74–5
levels of 67–8
nature of 71–3
skills 43
Kosovo
competencies 28

learning canopy
application of 89
common elements 89–91
deeper understanding 86–8
integrated approach to 88–9, 99
learning and subjects 82–6
organizational structures, for teaching 91–3
and specialism 93–4
learning futures *149*
learning process 111
learning skills 32–5
life skills 42–3
local contexts 117–26
application 121–2
community 123–5
local needs and opportunities 118–21
national expectations in 117–18
outside learning 122–3
student voice 125–6

Marton and Saljo model 69–70
Michelin starred restaurant (example) 21, 38

national curriculum 1–2, 9, 22
and curriculum design 9–10
response to economic and social changes 26–8
and school curriculum 2–3, 10, 14
of Singapore 13
see also English National Curriculum

National Qualifications Framework (NQF) 29
New Zealand 84
  competencies 27
  curriculum framework 40
  subject list 85
  subjects and learning 83

Office for Standards in Education, Children's
    Services and Skills (Ofsted) 18, 122–3
Olympic Games (example) 39–40, 46–7
Oxford, Cambridge and RSA examination boards
    (OCR)
  key skills 30

part-time work 153–4
pathways and gateways 139–54
  business and industrial requirements 147–8
  part-time work 153–4
  qualifications see qualifications
  vocational training 144–7
  vocational training, impact of 148–50
  work experiences see work experiences
Performance Indicators of Student Attainment
    (PISA) 185
Personal, Learning and Thinking Skills
    (PLTS) 11–12, 41
personal development 11, 31–2
personalisation, of learning 70
Peters, R. S. 85
Pink Strings (example) 153–4
POST (Pupil Online Survey Tool) 188

qualifications 140–1
  classification and identification of 141–2
  and design 144
  determining schools' offer 143
Qualifications and Credit Framework (QCF) 29
Qualifications and Curriculum Authority
    (QCA) 23, 24, 31, 33

restructure (example) 177
Revised Code of 1905 22
Rose Review (2010) 28, 29, 33
routines, of schools 14
Rumsfeld, Donald 125

satisfaction level (example) 96
schemata 101
school curriculum 2–3, 9, 10, 14, 15
school day extension 194–5
school leadership 178, 181
schools-within-a-school approach 180, 196
school year extension 194
sessions length 133–4
Sinek, Simon 17–18

Singapore
  curriculum framework 39, 43
  subject list 85
  '21st Century Competencies' 13, 24, 27, 42
skills 31, 101
  complexity of 166–8
  contexts for 168
  and deep learning 73–4
  definition of 12
  functional skills 28–9, 35
  key skills 11–12, 33, 34
  OCR key skills 30
  thinking and learning skills 32–5
skills links 87
social development 11
specialism 93–4
Specialist Schools and Academies Trust
    (SSAT) 70
stage-based classes arrangement 195–6
statue (example) 7, 18–19
students
  curriculum experience 9
  imagination 110
student voice 125–6
  and institutional management 187–8
  surveys 188–90
studio schools 144–5
subjects
  defined 84–6
  and learning 82–4
  list of 84
subject skills 76–9
successful learner 23–5

Tapscott, Don 148
teacher–student relationship 193
teaching
  and curriculum 58–9
  organizational structures for 91–3
technology, and vocational training 146–7
thinking skills 32–5
three-circle (Why, How, What) approach 17–18
3Cs 36–7, 37
timetable 90–1, 127–38
  and curriculum model 130–4
  dear timetabler 136–8
  design considerations 134
  example 127–8
  flexibility in 135–6, 180, 196–7
  key questions for 129–30
  models 135–6
  pressures on 128–9
twenty-first century curriculum 21–38
  basic skills 35–6
  in England 28–30

learning requirements in 23–5
learning requirements in, around the world 25–6
personality development 31–2
response to 26–8, 30–1
thinking and learning skills 32–5
   see also individual entries

understanding, definition of 12
United Nations Educational, Scientific and
   Cultural Organisation (UNESCO) 27, 159
'21st Century Competencies' 33
university technical colleges 144, 145

variable day 132–3
Victoria
   curriculum design 26
   'DNA' helix model 43, *44*
Victorian film-makers (example) 80

vocational training 144–5
   impact on curriculum 148–50
   and teaching approaches 145
   and technology 146–7
   work environment considerations 146

week-long lesson (example) 191
Wolf Report 141
work experience 150–1
   emphasizing ex students' achievements 152–3
   exclusion from offer 151
   individual 151
   small and medium sized businesses 151–2
work skills passport 157–8
world-class curriculum 198–200
   principles of 199

Young Enterprise Scheme 150